11+ MATHS
PRACTICE EXERCISES

David E Hanson

GALORE PARK

www.galorepark.co.uk

Published by Galore Park Publishing Ltd
338 Euston Road, London
NW1 3BH

www.galorepark.co.uk

Typesetting by DTP Media Ltd
Technical illustrations by DTP Media Ltd

Printed in Spain

ISBN 978 1 905735 92 1

First published 2014

Details of other Galore Park publications are available at www.galorepark.co.uk

About the author

David Hanson has over 40 years' experience of teaching and has been leader of the Independent Schools Examinations Board (ISEB) 11+ Maths setting team, a member of the ISEB 13+ Maths setting team and a member of the ISEB Editorial Endorsement Committee.

Acknowledgements

I would like to thank the reviewers of my early manuscript for their constructive suggestions, Louise Martine and the team at Galore Park for their support and help and Caitlin Grant for her assistance at all stages in the production of this book.

CONTENTS

INTRODUCTION

This book has been designed as a resource for the practice of basic skills and recall of knowledge.

The syllabus and examinations

Examination syllabuses, such as those for the ISEB 11+ and the Kent Test, are based upon

● the Programme of Study for Key Stage 2 of the National Curriculum, and
● the Framework for the National Numeracy Strategy up to, and including, Year 6

The National Curriculum and examination syllabuses are revised from time to time and it is important to be aware of the latest arrangements.

It is a good idea to

● find out about any expectations or requirements of a target school
● do additional practice on copies of recent past examination papers.

For completeness, and for the interest of high achievers, a little of the material covered in this book may be outside the requirements of current syllabuses.

The questions

Questions are numbered either

1.01 (a)

   (b)   where parts of the question are not related

or

1.01 (i)

   (ii)   where parts of the question are related.

Questions have been arranged in order of increasing complexity wherever possible, so pupils should feel a natural sense of progression as they work through the book.

Some questions are more demanding than the rest and are highlighted orange. For example: 3.07 , (a) , (i) . In tackling these questions, pupils may need to think more laterally and employ creative solutions to problems.

> ### Challenge 1A
>
> Challenge exercises, found in these orange boxes, are starting points for extension work. In attempting these exercises, pupils should explore possibilities, analyse patterns and record their working in greater detail than normal. A methodical approach should be encouraged, but also an appreciation of the power of numbers. Challenge exercises are a fun and interesting way to develop investigative skills and deeper understanding.

Calculators

It is assumed that calculators will not be used.

Marks

All of the numbered questions have a total of 6 marks, for consistency. A selection of 17 questions would have a total of 102 marks, which is conveniently close to 100, the total mark for each exam paper.

In general, each part question is allocated 1 mark. When two or more responses are required (as in writing the next few terms of a sequence), a student who has fully understood should be able to provide all the necessary responses. It is left to the discretion of those marking work to award a half mark for an incomplete, or partially correct, answer if this is considered appropriate.

In questions which are particularly time-consuming, or where a 'method' mark might reasonably be given, a part question may be allocated 2 marks.

How to use this book

While tackling the questions you are encouraged to

- look at things in different ways
- look for patterns
- ask questions – 'What if …?', 'How …?', 'When …?'

Answers to the questions are not included in this book; a separate answer book (9781905735938) is available.

Free downloadable worksheets are available where graphs or grids are required for some questions. Look for the W icon, which indicates a worksheet is available. The worksheets are available from www.galorepark.co.uk

USEFUL RESOURCES

11+ Maths Revision Guide by David E Hanson, ISBN 9781905735761

11+ English Revision Guide by Susan Hamlyn, ISBN 9781905735587

1 NUMBER

1.1 PROPERTIES OF NUMBERS

Questions involving

- types of number, including negative numbers
- the language of the four basic operations with numbers
- sequences
- multiples and factors
- prime numbers
- square numbers and square roots
- cube numbers and cube roots

1.01 (i)   How many dots are there in the box below? (1)

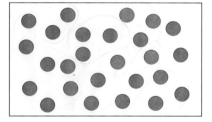

How many dots would there be if there were

(ii)   14 fewer (1)

(iii) 19 more (1)

(iv) twice as many (1)

(v)   half the number? (1)

(vi) If loops were drawn around groups of three dots, how many loops would be drawn and how many dots would be left outside the loops? (1)

Challenge 1A

Roll two ordinary dice.

Using the scores on the dice, write down a two digit number so that:

- the smaller score becomes the tens digit
- the larger score becomes the units digit.

Using the dice rolled on the right, the number made would be 16

(If the scores are the same, then you write down the multiple of 11)

You might like to change the instructions so that the larger score becomes the tens digit!

To investigate the idea in question 1.01 (vi) further, you could prepare a number of dots to draw loops round, or gather small stones or centimetre cubes to group together, or you could simply imagine a number of things.

Roll one die again to get a number other than 1 which will be the number of dots to be put in each loop, or the number of stones or cubes to be put in each group.

Write down (i) the number of groups and (ii) the number left out, if any.

1.02 (a) Erin counted the ladybirds on a bush in her garden at midday each day one weekend and recorded the numbers as a pictogram using her computer.

Saturday	🐞 🐞 🐞 🐞 🐞 🐞 🐞 🐞 🐞 🐞 🐞
Sunday	🐞 🐞 🐞 🐞 🐞 🐞 🐞

Key: 🐞 represents 1 ladybird.

(i) How many ladybirds did Erin count on Saturday? (1)

(ii) How many fewer ladybirds did she count on Sunday than she counted on Saturday? (1)

(iii) What was the average (mean) number of ladybirds counted on one day? (1)

(b) This drawing shows a number of shapes on a tray.

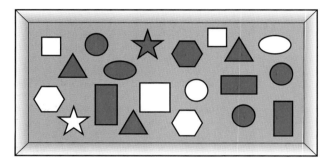

(i) How many dark shapes are there? (1)

(ii) How many shapes are there altogether? (1)

(iii) How many more dark shapes are there than light shapes? (1)

1.03 Copy and complete these statements using the words **odd** and **even**.

(i) An even number plus an odd number is always an _____ number. (1)

(ii) An even number minus an _____ number is always an odd number. (1)

(iii) An odd number plus an _____ number is always an odd number. (1)

(iv) An even number multiplied by an even number is always an _____ number. (1)

(v) An _____ number times an _____ number is always an odd number. (1)

(vi) If an even number divides exactly by an odd number, the result is always an _____ number. (1)

Challenge 1B

You need a set of nine number cards 1 to 9 and a coin with a label marked E on one side and a label marked O on the other side.

Choose 3 number cards and toss the coin.

Combine any two of the three cards by addition, subtraction or multiplication to give the largest number – odd or even, as indicated by the coin.

For example, here the largest even number would be 32 (4 × 8).
The largest odd number would have been 11 (3 + 8).

You could change the rule so that you:
● find the smallest number instead of the largest – in the example the smallest even number is 4 (unless you allow division in which case the smallest is 2), and the smallest odd number is 1
● combine all three cards – in the example, the largest even number is 96 and the largest odd number is 35

1.04 (a) Two identical thermometers show the temperatures, in °C, inside and outside Tommy's window.

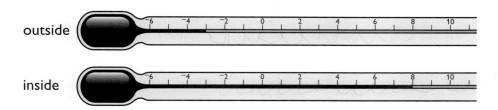

outside

inside

    (i)   What is the temperature inside the window? (1)

    (ii)   What is the temperature outside the window? (1)

    (iii)   How many degrees colder is it outside than inside? (1)

(b) Jennie keeps a record of the temperatures inside and outside her window at midday. On 1 June the temperature outside was 24 °C and the temperature inside was 7 degrees lower.

    (i)   What was the inside temperature? (1)

On 1 January the temperature outside was ⁻4 °C and the temperature inside was 19 degrees higher.

    (ii)   What was the temperature inside? (1)

During February, the maximum outside temperature was 8 °C and the minimum outside temperature was ⁻11 °C.

    (iii)   What was the difference between these temperatures? (1)

1.05 (a) Helen is swimming. She dives to ⁻2.5 m (2.5 metres below the water surface) and looks up at a jellyfish 1.8 m above her. At what depth is the jellyfish swimming? (2)

(b) When Robbie sets off from a car park to climb a mountain, the temperature is 10 °C. As he climbs, the temperature falls. At the top of the mountain, the temperature is 13 degrees lower than the temperature at the car park. What is the temperature at the top of the mountain? (1)

(c) Jasmine owes Rachel £5, Rachel owes Alfie £3 and Alfie owes Jasmine £7

None of them has any money until Alfie's mother gives him £10

When they have all repaid their debts, how much will each of them have? (3)

1.06 Copy and complete the following.

    (i)   11 + 6 = _____ (1)

    (ii)   18 − 9 = _____ (1)

    (iii)   11 × 5 = _____ (1)

    (iv)   28 ÷ 7 = _____ (1)

    (v)   ⁻3 + ⁻7 = _____ (1)

    (vi)   8 − ⁻5 = _____ (1)

1.07 (a) (i) On a copy of the number track below, write the numbers 23 and 30 in the correct boxes. (1)

			25	26						33	

(ii) Which number lies exactly half way between 25 and 31? (1)

(b) (i) On a copy of the number track below, write the numbers ⁻2 and 5 in the correct boxes. (1)

	⁻5				0		3			

(ii) Which number lies exactly halfway between ⁻5 and 1? (1)

(c) On a copy of the number track below, write in every third number. (1)

8			5									

(d) On a copy of the number track below, write in every third number. (1)

⁻0.4			0.2								

1.08 (a) (i) Count forwards four more steps, in fours from 31

23   27   31   …   …   …   … (1)

(ii) Count backwards four more steps, in sixes from 88

100   94   88   …   …   …   … (1)

(b) Copy these 'counting on' or 'counting back' sequences and write the next four terms of each one.

(i)   1   5   9   13   17   …   …   …   … (1)

(ii)   53   46   39   32   25   …   …   …   … (1)

(iii)   8.8   9.0   9.2   9.4   9.6   …   …   …   … (1)

(iv)   1.4   1.1   0.8   0.5   0.2   …   …   …   … (1)

1.09 Copy these sequences and write the next two terms of each one.

(i)   13   18   23   28   33   …   … (1)

(ii)   200   191   182   173   164   …   … (1)

(iii)   20   25   30   35   40   …   … (1)

(iv)   27   33   39   45   51   …   … (1)

(v)   59   55   51   47   43   …   … (1)

(vi)   288   144   72   36   18   …   … (1)

1.10 Copy these sequences and for each one write the next two terms.

(i)   4   7   10   13   ...   ...   (1)

(ii)   1   2   4   8   ...   ...   (1)

(iii) 1   3   9   27   ...   ...   (1)

(iv) 16   8   4   2   ...   ...   (1)

(v)   1   5   9   13   ...   ...   (1)

(vi) 1000 100   10   1   ...   ...   (1)

1.11 Copy these sequences and write the missing numbers in the gaps.

(i)   ____   43   47   ____   55   ____   (1)

(ii)   ____ $^-3$ ____   3   6   ____   (1)

(iii) 108   ____   84   72   ____   48   (1)

(iv) 1   ____   7   ____   31   ____   (1)

(v)   3   ____   10   15   ____   ____   (1)

(vi) ____   2   4   7   11   ____   (1)

1.12 Draw the next two patterns in each of these sequences and write the number of circles under each pattern.

(i)   (2)

(ii)   (2)

(iii)   (2)

1.13 Copy these sequences and for each one write the next two numbers.

(i)   1   4   10   22   ...   ...   (1)

(ii)   1   3   2   4   3   5   ...   ...   (1)

(iii) 1   2   3   5   8   13   ...   ...   (1)

(iv) 33   34   17   18   9   10   5   ...   ...   (1)

(v)   1   2   5   10   17   ...   ...   (1)

(vi) 4   10   9   15   14   20   19   ...   ...   (1)

1.14 Copy these sequences and for each one write the next two numbers.

(i) ⁻47   ⁻36   ⁻25   ⁻14   ⁻3   …   …   (1)

(ii) 17   13   9   5   1   …   …   (1)

(iii) 1   2   5   14   41   …   …   (1)

(iv) 1   4   5   9   14   …   …   (1)

(v) 2   4   8   14   22   …   …   (1)

(vi) 9   19   18   28   27   …   …   (1)

1.15 Copy these sequences and for each one write the next two numbers.

(i) 10   7   4   1   …   …   (1)

(ii) 162   54   18   6   …   …   (1)

(iii) 2   2   4   6   …   …   (1)

(iv) 3   7   12   18   …   …   (1)

(v) $\frac{1}{2}$ $\frac{2}{4}$ $\frac{3}{6}$ $\frac{4}{8}$ …   …   (1)

(vi) 1   4   9   16   …   …   (1)

1.16 (i)   On a copy of the number grid below, shade in 3 and then every third number.   (2)

W 2

1	2	3	4	5	6
7	8	9	10	11	12
13	14	15	16	17	18
19	20	21	22	23	24
25	26	27	28	29	30
31	32	33	34	35	36

(ii)   On your copy, put a cross ✗ on 4 and then every fourth number.   (2)

(iii)   What can you say about the numbers which are shaded and have a cross?   (2)

1.17 (a) Two frogs, Flip and Flop are playing a game on a strip of 50 squares.

S	1	2	3	4	5	6	7	8	9	10	11	12	13	14	15	16

They both start on the square marked **S**.

Flip can leap over three squares so he lands first on 4

(i) On a copy of the diagram above (which shows the first 16 squares), put a cross on all the squares he will land on. (1)

Flop is not as agile as Flip! She can only leap over two squares.

(ii) On your copy, shade all the squares she will land on. (1)

(iii) List the numbers of all the squares less than 50 which both frogs will land on. (1)

(iv) What do you notice about these numbers? (1)

(b) Sally and John are playing a clapping game. They both start clapping at 12:00 exactly. Sally claps every 30 seconds and John claps every 40 seconds.

At what time will they next clap at exactly the same time? (2)

1.18 Copy these statements and for each one write **true** or **false**.

(i) Every even multiple of 3 is divisible by 6 (1)

(ii) All multiples of 6 are even. (1)

(iii) Every number ending in 0 or 5 is divisible by 5 (1)

(iv) All multiples of 4 are also multiples of 8 (1)

(v) Every number which has 2 as a factor is even. (1)

(vi) All multiples of 9 have a digit sum of 9 (1)

Challenge 1C

From a set of nine number cards 1 to 9, choose 3 cards at random.

Example: 6 7 2

Set yourself (or a friend) a challenge.

Example: Place the cards side by side to make

(i) the largest possible multiple of 3
For these cards, this is 762 (762 has a digit sum of 15 which is divisible by 3).

(ii) the largest possible factor of 96
For these cards, this is 6

You can be as adventurous as you wish, for example:
Choose 5 cards at random.

Example: 5 9 4 8 2

(iii) Make the largest possible multiple of 3
For these cards, this is 9852 (9852 has a digit sum of 24 which is divisible by 3).

(iv) Make the largest possible factor of 96
For these cards, this is 48

1.19 In Watermeadows School, each classroom has eight tables which can each seat up to four pupils. Ideally, the pupils are seated in groups of equal size.

(i) Miss Grant's class has 12 pupils. They have been told to group themselves in fours around tables.

How else could Miss Grant's class have been put into groups of equal size? (1)

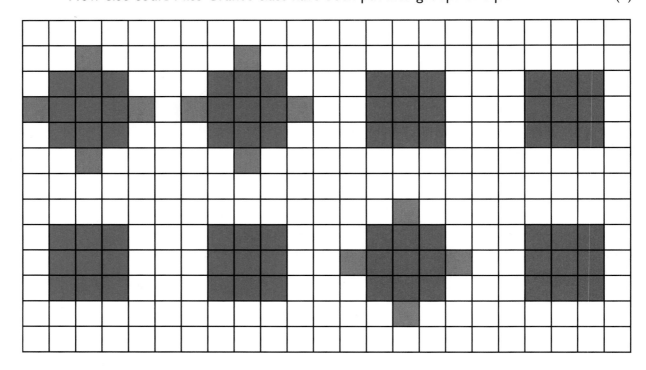

(ii) Which two other class sizes between (and including) 12 and 20 could be grouped in fours? (1)

(iii) Mr Brown's class has 18 pupils. How could they best be grouped? (1)

(iv) Miss Chilwan's class has 19 pupils. Why is it not possible to arrange this class in groups of equal size? (1)

(v) List the possible ways that Miss Chilwan's class can be seated with no fewer than three pupils at a table. (2)

1.20 (a) Which of the following numbers are divisible by 5? (1)

15   25   40   75   120 400 3050

(b) Which of the following numbers are divisible by 3? (1)

16   36   42   98   102   301   1011

(c) Which of the following numbers are divisible by 6? (1)

18   24   32   54   78   102 2100

(d) Which of the following numbers are divisible by 9? (1)

18   27   56   72   108   117 2106

(e) Which of the following numbers are divisible by 7? (2)

21   45   63   82   98   217 749

1.21 In each part of this question, make a copy of the list of numbers.

  (i)   Circle the multiples of 4   (1)

      8   14   20   28   30   42   48   52   60

  (ii) Circle the multiples of 7   (2)

      14   27   35   42   54   56   63   77   91

  (iii) Circle the factors of 48   (2)

      2   3   4   5   6   7   8   9   10   11   12

  (iv) Circle the factors of 100   (1)

      1   2   3   4   5   6   7   8   9   10   11   12

1.22 (a) (i)   List all the factors of 12   (2)

         (ii) List all the factors of 27   (1)

         (iii) Which numbers are factors of both 12 and 27?   (1)

     (b) List, in order, the eight integers which are factors of 30   (2)

1.23 (a) Two of the factor pairs of 32 are 1 and 32, and 2 and 16

     By drawing a factor rainbow, or otherwise, write down another factor pair of 32   (1)

     (b) (i)   List all of the factor pairs of 64   (1)

         (ii) What special feature is there in the factors of a square number?   (1)

     (c) Giving an example, explain what is special about the factor pairs of prime numbers.   (1)

     (d) What is the smallest number with four factor pairs?   (2)

1.24 The multiplication grid below has been partially completed.

×	2	3	4	5	6	7	8	9
2							16	
3			12					
4				28				
5								45
6			30					
7		21						
8				48				
9	18							

  W2

  (i)   On a copy of the grid, shade in all the squares representing multiples of 7   (2)

  (ii) On your copy, write all the square numbers in the correct places.   (2)

  (iii) If you were to complete the square, how many times would you write the number 12?   (2)

1.25 (a) Ahmed has drawn the Carroll diagram below and plans to write the integers 1 to 20 inclusive in the correct regions.

	multiple of 3	not a multiple of 3
not a multiple of 5		
multiple of 5		

Which numbers should Ahmed write

(i)   in the grey region   (1)

(ii)   in the orange region?   (2)

(b) Celia has drawn the Carroll diagram below and plans to write the integers 1 to 20 inclusive in the correct regions.

	factor of 24	not a factor of 24
not a factor of 30		
factor of 30		

Which numbers should Celia write

(i)   in the grey region   (1)

(ii)   in the orange region?   (2)

1.26 (a) Here are the first four multiples of 3 represented by patterns of circles:

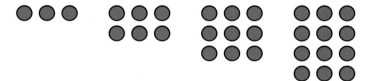

Notice that the first multiple of 3 is 3

Draw similar patterns to represent the next two multiples of 3 and write the number of circles under each pattern.   (2)

(b) Here are the first three square numbers represented by patterns of circles:

Draw similar patterns to represent the next two square numbers and write the number of circles under each pattern.   (2)

(c) You will notice in parts (a) and (b) that the third multiple of 3 is the square of 3

What is

(i)   the fifth multiple of 5   (1)

(ii)   the seventh multiple of 7?   (1)

1.27 The grid below shows an arrangement of the counting numbers in order.

			1	2	3
4	5	6	7	8	9
10	11	12	13	14	15
16	17	18	19	20	21
22	23	24	25	26	27
28	29	30	31	32	33

(i)   What do you notice about the numbers in the column shaded grey?   (1)

(ii)   On a copy of the grid, complete the next two rows.   (1)

The first three prime numbers, 2, 3 and 5, are shaded.

(iii)   On your copy, shade all the other prime numbers.   (1)

(iv)   What do you notice about the positions of the prime numbers except 2 and 3?   (1)

Shanna suggests that every prime number might be 1 more or 1 less than a multiple of 6

73 is a prime number.

(v)   Divide 73 by 6 and say what you notice.   (2)

Challenge 1D

You might like to carry out an investigation to see if Shanna's idea holds true for other prime numbers.

1.28 (a)   (i)   List the six factors of 12   (1)

(ii)   List the factors of 12 which are prime numbers.   (1)

(iii)   Write 12 as a product of its prime factors.   (1)

(b)   (i)   List the factors of 21   (1)

(ii)   List the factors of 21 which are prime numbers.   (1)

(iii)   Write 21 as a product of its prime factors.   (1)

1.29 (a)   List the prime factors of

(i)   24   (1)

(ii)   42   (1)

(iii)   81   (1)

(b)   Write each of these numbers as a product of its prime factors.

(i)   24   (1)

(ii)   54   (1)

(iii)   100   (1)

1.30 Six numbers have been written as the product of their prime factors.

In each case, say what the number is.

(i) $2 \times 5 \times 7$ (1)

(ii) $2 \times 2 \times 3 \times 11$ (1)

(iii) $3 \times 13 \times 17$ (1)

(iv) $2^2 \times 3 \times 5^2$ (1)

(v) $2^3 \times 7^2$ (1)

(vi) $2 \times 3 \times 5 \times 7 \times 11$ (1)

1.31 The drawings below show models of cube numbers.

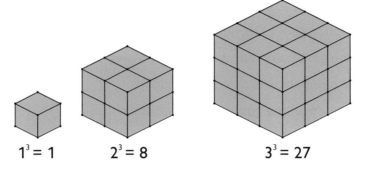

$1^3 = 1$ $\qquad$ $2^3 = 8$ $\qquad$ $3^3 = 27$

(i) On isometric dotted paper, draw similar pictures to show models of the next two cube numbers. (2)

(ii) What is the sixth cube number? (1)

(iii) What is the seventh cube number? (1)

(iv) How many cube numbers are there that are smaller than a million? (2)

1.32 Here is a number sequence:

4 8 12 16 20 24 28 32 36 40 44 48

From the number sequence, write down

(i) all the square numbers (1)

(ii) a cube number (1)

(iii) all the multiples of 8 (1)

(iv) all the factors of 60 (1)

(v) two numbers with a product of 80 (1)

(vi) two numbers with a difference of 44 (1)

1.33 Seven number cards are shown below.

| 2 | 15 | 16 | 48 | 11 | 4 | 27 |

From the list write down

(i)	two prime numbers	(1)
(ii)	two square numbers	(1)
(iii)	a multiple of 24	(1)
(iv)	a factor of 33	(1)
(v)	a cube number	(1)
(vi)	the cube root of 64	(1)

1.34 From the numbers

3   7   9   14   90

write down

(i)	two factors of 56	(1)
(ii)	a square number	(1)
(iii)	all the prime numbers	(1)
(iv)	the number which is a common multiple of 2 and 5	(1)
(v)	three numbers which have a sum of 30	(1)
(vi)	the square root of 49	(1)

Challenge 1E

You might like to use the ideas in this section to make up puzzles for your friends. For example, 'Which number below 50 has a cube root which is 1 less than a square number?'

With practice you will be able to ask, and answer, more difficult questions. For example: 'Which number below 50 is a multiple of 7 and 3 more than a square number?'

1.2 PLACE VALUE AND ORDERING

Questions involving

- reading and writing numbers
- place value
- comparing and ordering numbers, including use of the number line
- using signs, including inequality signs

1.35 A number is shown on the abacus below.

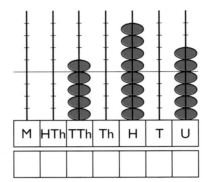

M	HTh	TTh	Th	H	T	U

    (i)   Write the number in figures.   (1)

    (ii)   Write the numbers in words.   (1)

 On blank copies of the abacus, show the number which is

    (iii)   187 larger than the number shown on the abacus above   (2)

    (iv)   187 smaller than the number shown on the abacus above.   (2)

Challenge 1F

 On blank copies of the abacus show five numbers less than 10 million which use three digit 3s, for example, 3 003 030

Write each number in words.

What is (i) the largest and (ii) the smallest of these numbers?

Think about the place value of each 3 in your numbers.

Is it true to say that all of these numbers are multiples of (iii) 3 and (iv) 6?

1.36 (a)   Write in numerals (figures) the numbers

        (i)   one thousand, four hundred and twelve   (1)

        (ii)   thirteen thousand, one hundred and one   (1)

        (iii)   five thousand and eleven.   (1)

    (b)   Write in words the numbers

        (i)   4050   (1)

        (ii)   30 149   (1)

        (iii)   104 503   (1)

1.37 Which number is shown on this abacus?

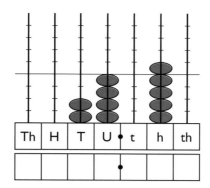

    (i)   Write the number in figures.   (1)

    (ii)   Write the numbers in words.   (1)

On blank copies of the abacus, show the number which is

    (iii)   0.98 larger than the number shown on the abacus above   (2)

    (iv)   0.98 smaller than the number shown on the abacus above.   (2)

1.38 The 4 in 1042 has the value 40 (4 tens).

What is the value of

    (i)   the 7 in 417   (1)

    (ii)   the 3 in 4312   (1)

    (iii)   the 6 in 206 100?   (1)

What is the value of

    (iv)   the 7 if 417 is multiplied by 100   (1)

    (v)   the 3 if 4312 is divided by 100   (1)

    (vi)   the 6 if 206 100 is multiplied by 100?   (1)

1.39 (a)   In the number 465.67, how many times greater is the orange 6 than the black 6?   (1)

    (b)   (i)   Copy these numbers and put a decimal point in each of them so that the 5 has a value of 5 tenths.   (1)

                    315   152   6053

       (ii)   Copy these numbers and put a decimal point in each of them so that the 3 has a value of 3 hundredths.   (2)

                    823   73   35

    (c)   How many times more than

       (i)   750 is 750 000   (1)

       (ii)   80.5 is 8050?   (1)

1.40 (a) Which of the following numbers have a digit zero of the same value? (2)

507   2010   70.6   0.34   1.09

(b) Which of the following numbers have a digit 7 of the same value? (2)

175   8745   0.7   7   370.5

(c) Which of the following numbers have a digit 5 of the same value? (2)

145   1 450 000   154 000   145 000   59 000   1 050 000

1.41 (a) On the number line below, the number 2 is shown as a red dot.

On a copy of the number line, mark and label clearly the number

(i) which is 3 less than 2 (1)

(ii) ⁻3 (1)

(b) On a different copy of the number line, show the numbers which are less than or equal to 3 (2)

(c) On a different copy of the number line, show the numbers x such that $⁻2 < x \leq 2$ (2)

Challenge 1G

You might like to play a game with a friend.
Make two spinners, A and B.

Player 1 spins spinner B and then spinner A. Then player 2 spins spinner B, hoping to get a number which satisfies the sign shown on spinner A. You can invent your own rules! You could make a new spinner B showing fractions!

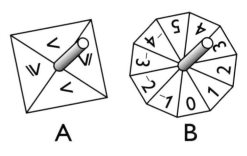

A   B

1.42 (a) You will need a copy of the number line below.

On your copy, mark and label clearly the numbers

(i) 7 (1)

(ii) 1.5 (1)

(iii) ⁻4 (1)

(b) On a different copy of the number line, mark and label clearly

(i) ⁻0.5 (1)

(ii) 1.8 (1)

(iii) 4.25 (1)

1.43 (a) Give an example of a number between

      (i)   55 and 65   (1)

      (ii)   6.5 and 7.0   (1)

      (iii) 0.1 and 0.2   (1)

  (b) Which number is exactly halfway between

      (i)   6 and 16   (1)

      (ii)   48 and 62   (1)

      (iii) 72 and 136?   (1)

1.44 (a) Write these numbers in order of **increasing** size.   (1)

      13   19   89   17   103

  (b) Write these numbers in order, starting with the **largest**.   (1)

      3.5   5.9   5.3   3.9   9.3

  (c) Write these numbers in order, the **smallest** first.   (1)

      543   354   534   345   453

  (d) Write these numbers in order of **decreasing** size.   (1)

      102   120   2010   1020   1201   1200

  (e) Write these numbers in order of **increasing** size.   (1)

      103 402   1 030 402   100 342   100 324   102 430

  (f) Write these numbers in order, starting with the **largest**.   (1)

      898 989   89 898   98 899   898 889   899 988

1.45 (a) Write these numbers in order of size, starting with the **smallest**.   (1)

      5.42   4.52   4.25   5.24   2.54

  (b) Write these numbers in order of size, starting with the **largest**.   (1)

      0.45   0.54   0.405   0.504   0.045

  (c) Write these numbers in order of size, starting with the **smallest**.   (1)

      7.02   7.2   7   7.202   7.021

  (d) Write these numbers in order of **decreasing** size.   (1)

      3.12   21.3   2.31   1.32   2.13

  (e) Write these numbers in order of **increasing** size.   (1)

      0.28   0.802   0.028   0.208   0.82

  (f) Write these numbers in order of size, starting with the **largest**.   (1)

      0.703   0.307   0.37   0.037   0.73

1.46 The table below shows the times, in seconds, recorded in a 100 metre running race.

Lane	1	2	3	4	5	6	7	8
Name	Archie	Bella	Clare	David	Edith	Francis	Gemma	Harriet
Time	13.59	14.12	13.25	13.05	14.20	13.61	13.14	12.69

(i) Copy, extend and complete the table below to show all eight children in order of finishing. (4)

Position	Name	Time (seconds)
1st		
2nd		

(ii) By how many seconds did the fastest beat the slowest? (2)

Challenge 1H

In our decimal (base 10) number system, we count in tens and use ten digits, 0, 1, 2, 3, 4, 5, 6, 7, 8 and 9
A decimal abacus has spikes to hold up to nine beads (see question 1.35 on page 14).

In the binary (base two) number system, we count in twos and use just two digits, 0 and 1
A binary abacus has spikes to hold only one bead. The number shown in the diagram below is the binary number 101 (5 in decimal).

eights	fours	twos	units
	1	0	1

(a) Draw abacus pictures like the one above to show all of the binary numbers from 1 to 1111 (15 in decimal).

(b) Using binary numbers, make up (and answer!) simple questions involving prime numbers, square numbers, sequences and ordering.

1.3 ESTIMATION AND APPROXIMATION

Questions involving

● estimation
● approximation, including decimal places and significant figures

1.47 (i) Estimate (do not count) the number of dots in the rectangle below. (2)

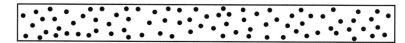

(ii) Now count the number of dots. (2)

(iii) How accurate was your estimate? Explain, or show, what you did. (2)

1.48 (a) Estimate the position of 2 on the number line below. On a copy of the line, mark it clearly with a cross. (2)

0   10

(b) Estimate the position of 60 on the number line below. On a copy of the line, mark it clearly with a cross. (2)

0   100

(c) Estimate the position of 800 on the number line below. On a copy of the line, mark it clearly with a cross. (2)

0   1000

1.49 (a) (i) Estimate (do not count) the number of circles in the pattern below. (2)

(ii) Explain how you did this. (2)

(b) Estimate (do not measure) the length of the slug in this picture. (2)

1.50 (a) Round

(i) 445 to the nearest ten (1)

(ii) 7049 to the nearest hundred (1)

(iii) 3499 to the nearest thousand. (1)

(b) Round the number 654.8 to the nearest

(i) whole number (1)

(ii) ten (1)

(iii) hundred. (1)

1.51 Nicole uses each of the digits 5, 1, 6 and 9 to make a four-digit number, for example 6195

(i) What is the smallest four-digit number she can make? (1)

(ii) Write your answer to part (i) correct to the nearest 1000 (1)

(iii) Write your answer to part (i) correct to the nearest 10 (1)

(iv) What is the largest four-digit number she can make? (1)

(v) Write your answer to part (iv) correct to the nearest 100 (1)

(vi) Write your answer to part (iv) correct to the nearest 1000 (1)

1.52 (a) When Aisha multiplies 5.8 by 3.7 she gets an answer of 21.46

Write this answer correct to the nearest

    (i)   whole number   (1)

    (ii)   tenth.   (1)

(b) The result of a calculation on William's calculator is   `4870.949`

Write this result correct to the nearest

    (i)   hundred   (1)

    (ii)   whole number   (1)

    (iii)   tenth   (1)

    (iv)   hundredth.   (1)

1.53 (a) The crowd at a rugby match was recorded as 34 449

Write this number to the nearest

    (i)   1000   (1)

    (ii)   100   (1)

    (iii)   10   (1)

(b) Estimate (do not calculate exactly) the result of the following calculations, giving your answers to 1 significant figure.

    (i) $1012 + 8994$ (1)

    (ii) $3107 - 1984$ (1)

    (iii) 205×99 (1)

1.54 (a) Write these numbers correct to 2 significant figures.

    (i)   385   (1)

    (ii)   12.4   (1)

    (iii)   0.548   (1)

(b) Write these numbers correct to 3 significant figures.

    (i)   404 590   (1)

    (ii)   0.058 39   (1)

    (iii)   34.99   (1)

1.55 (a) Write these numbers correct to 1 decimal place.

    (i)   4.45   (1)

    (ii)   7.549   (1)

    (iii)   11.55   (1)

(b) Write these numbers correct to 2 decimal places.

    (i)   7.936   (1)

    (ii)   0.048 03   (1)

    (iii)   12.995   (1)

Challenge 1I

You will have noticed the horizontal line above 4 beads on the abacus diagrams (for example on page 15). This is an aid to rounding numbers.

Rounding 1549 to the nearest hundred:

- Draw, or imagine, a vertical line to the right of the hundreds column.
- Look at the column immediately to the right of the vertical line.
- If, in that column (the tens column, in this case), there were beads above the horizontal line, then we would round up, but there are not, so we round down.

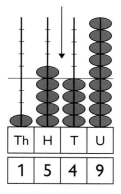 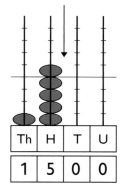

Th	H	T	U
1	5	4	9

Th	H	T	U
1	5	0	0

So 1549 rounded to the nearest hundred is 1500

Look again at questions 1.50 to 1.55 and draw or imagine abacus pictures.

1.56 (a)   The diagram below shows a garden. Estimate the proportion which is lawn.   (2)

patio	lawn

(b)   Emily estimates that her pencil gets about half a centimetre shorter every school day. On Monday morning, the length of her pencil is 15.9 cm and Emily considers the pencil too short to use when it is about 8 cm long.

Estimate

(i)   the length of her pencil after classes on Friday   (1)

(ii)   the number of school days that she will be able to use the pencil before it becomes too short.   (1)

(c)   Becky can complete about six lines of neat handwriting in one minute. There are about 35 lines on each page of her English exercise book. Estimate how long it will take her to write a ten-page story.   (2)

1.57 (a)   Sam has taken about 40 minutes to read the 19 pages in the first chapter of a novel which has 395 pages.

(i)   Estimate how many hours, to the nearest hour, it will take Sam to read the whole book.   (2)

(ii)   Explain how you did this.   (1)

(b)   (i)   Estimate the length, in centimetres, of this piece of wool.   (2)

(ii)   Explain how you did this.   (1)

1.4 FRACTIONS, DECIMALS, PERCENTAGES AND RATIO

Questions involving

- proper fractions, including equivalent fractions and simplest form (lowest terms)
- comparing and ordering fractions
- improper fractions and mixed numbers
- operations with fractions
- equivalence of fractions, decimals and percentages
- ratio and proportion
- fractional and percentage parts of quantities

1.58 What fractions, in their simplest form, of these rectangles have been shaded?

(i) (1)

(ii) (1)

(iii) (1)

(iv) (1)

(v) (1)

(vi) (1)

1.59 (a) For each of the diagrams below, say what fraction, in its simplest form, is shaded.

(i)  (1)

(ii)  (1)

(iii)  (1)

(iv) 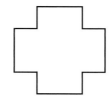 (1)

(b) Copy this shape and shade $\frac{3}{4}$ of it. (1)

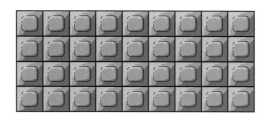

(c) Draw a square and shade about $\frac{1}{3}$ of it. (1)

1.60 (a) The diagram below shows a chocolate bar with 36 pieces.

How many pieces will there be in

(i) $\frac{3}{4}$ of the bar (1)

(ii) $\frac{2}{3}$ of the bar (1)

(iii) $\frac{5}{6}$ of the bar? (1)

(b) Sally baked a cake on Friday. She and a friend each ate $\frac{1}{8}$ of it straight away. On Saturday, her sister ate a third of what was left.

(i) What fraction of the whole cake did her sister eat? (2)

(ii) What fraction of the whole cake remained? (1)

1.61 (a) Trevor had a box containing 20 chocolates. He gave Trisha a fifth of them.

      (i)   How many chocolates did Trisha get? (1)

    Trevor then dropped the box and a quarter of the remaining chocolates fell out and had to be thrown away.

      (ii)   What fraction, in its simplest form, of the 20 chocolates was left? (1)

  (b) Thomasina, Dixie and Harriet shared a pizza. They cut the pizza into eight equal slices. Thomasina and Dixie each had one slice and Harriet had two slices.

      (i)   Draw a circle to represent the whole pizza and then draw and label each portion. (1)

      (ii)   What fraction of the whole pizza was left? (1)

    The three friends decided to share the rest of the pizza equally between them.

      (iii) What would be the best way that they could do this? (1)

      (iv) How many of the eight original slices did Harriet eat altogether? (1)

1.62 Elizabeth is reading a book which has 320 pages.

One day, she read $\frac{1}{8}$ of the book.

  (i)   How many pages did she read? (1)

The next day, she read another 64 pages.

  (ii)   What fraction of the book, in its simplest form, is 64 pages? (2)

  (iii) What fraction of the book has Elizabeth now read altogether? (2)

  (iv) How many pages has she left to read? (1)

1.63 (a) What is $\frac{2}{3}$ of 78 kg? (2)

  (b) $\frac{2}{3}$ of a loaf of bread has been eaten. Six slices remain. How many slices were in the loaf? (2)

  (c) Morag buys 1 m of elastic. When it is stretched, it is $1\frac{1}{4}$ times as long. How long is the piece of elastic when it is stretched? (1)

  (d) The price of a laptop was originally £450 but the price has been reduced by £150

    By what fraction of the original price has the laptop been reduced? (1)

1.64 (a) Billy ate $\frac{3}{5}$ of a cake. What fraction of the cake was left? (1)

  (b) Bertie's aunt gave him £80 and asked him to save $\frac{4}{5}$ of it. How much did she ask Bertie to save? (1)

  (c) Each of Elsie's five cats eats $1\frac{1}{2}$ sachets of cat food each day. How many sachets of cat food would be required to feed all five cats? (2)

  (d) Amy and Beatrice have a new packet of sweets. The label says that there are between 40 and 50 sweets in the packet. Amy eats exactly a third of the sweets and Beatrice eats exactly a fifth of the sweets. How many sweets were in the packet? (2)

1.65 (a)   Sarah has drawn a machine which finds equivalent fractions.

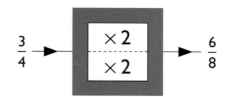

In the diagram above, the machine is changing $\frac{3}{4}$ into eighths.

Using blank copies of the machine, show how the machine can change

(i) $\frac{1}{2}$ into tenths   (1)

(ii) $\frac{2}{3}$ into twelfths.   (1)

(b)   Change

(i) $\frac{2}{5}$ into tenths   (1)

(ii) $\frac{3}{4}$ into twentieths.   (1)

(c)   Showing how you do this, find which is larger:

(i) $\frac{4}{5}$ or $\frac{17}{20}$ (1)

(ii) $\frac{4}{5}$ or $\frac{3}{4}$ (1)

1.66 (a)   Donald has drawn a machine which simplifies fractions.

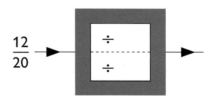

Using a blank copy of the machine, show how the machine can change $\frac{12}{20}$ to its simplest form (lowest terms).   (1)

(b)   Write the following fractions in their simplest form.

(i) $\frac{9}{12}$ (1)

(ii) $\frac{16}{20}$ (1)

(iii) $\frac{14}{16}$ (1)

(iv) $\frac{5}{40}$ (1)

(v) $\frac{18}{30}$ (1)

1.67 (a) Of the fractions below, which is

   (i)   the smallest   (1)

   (ii)   the biggest?   (1)

$$\frac{1}{4} \quad \frac{1}{3} \quad \frac{1}{6} \quad \frac{1}{8} \quad \frac{1}{5} \quad \frac{1}{10}$$

(b) Which is bigger:

   (i) $\frac{4}{5}$ or $\frac{7}{10}$?   (1)

   (ii) $\frac{3}{4}$ or $\frac{2}{3}$?   (1)

(c) Write these fractions in order of increasing size.   (2)

$$\frac{1}{3} \quad \frac{3}{4} \quad \frac{1}{2} \quad \frac{2}{3} \quad \frac{1}{4}$$

1.68 You will need a copy of the number line below.

On your copy, mark with crosses and label clearly

   (i) $\frac{1}{2}$ (1)

   (ii) $\frac{1}{4}$ (1)

   (iii) $\frac{3}{4}$ (1)

   (iv) $\frac{2}{3}$ (1)

   (v) $1\frac{1}{4}$ (1)

   (vi) $\frac{5}{6}$ (1)

1.69 (a) How many halves are there in $2\frac{1}{2}$?   (1)

(b) How many quarters are there in $3\frac{1}{4}$?   (1)

(c) Write the following mixed numbers as improper fractions.

   (i) $1\frac{3}{4}$ (1)

   (ii) $2\frac{2}{3}$ (1)

   (iii) $3\frac{4}{5}$ (1)

   (iv) $4\frac{3}{7}$ (1)

1.70 Write the following improper fractions as mixed numbers.

(i) $\frac{5}{2}$ (1)

(ii) $\frac{5}{3}$ (1)

(iii) $\frac{12}{5}$ (1)

(iv) $\frac{15}{4}$ (1)

(v) $\frac{17}{3}$ (1)

(vi) $\frac{18}{7}$ (1)

1.71 Setting out your work clearly, to show what you are doing, carry out the following additions.

(i) $\frac{1}{2} + \frac{1}{3}$ (1)

(ii) $\frac{1}{3} + \frac{3}{4}$ (1)

(iii) $\frac{1}{2} + \frac{3}{5}$ (1)

(iv) $\frac{1}{4} + \frac{1}{6}$ (1)

(v) $\frac{7}{8} + \frac{3}{16}$ (1)

(vi) $1\frac{1}{2} + 2\frac{5}{8}$ (1)

1.72 Setting out your work clearly, to show what you are doing, carry out the following subtractions.

(i) $\frac{1}{2} - \frac{1}{3}$ (1)

(ii) $\frac{2}{3} - \frac{1}{4}$ (1)

(iii) $\frac{1}{2} - \frac{2}{5}$ (1)

(iv) $\frac{1}{4} - \frac{1}{6}$ (1)

(v) $\frac{7}{8} - \frac{11}{16}$ (1)

(vi) $1\frac{1}{2} - \frac{4}{5}$ (1)

Challenge 1J

$\boxed{\begin{smallmatrix}W\\13\end{smallmatrix}}$ From centimetre squared paper, cut a strip of 12 squares. This will represent one whole.

Now make the following fraction strips:

$\frac{1}{12}$ 1 square $\frac{1}{6}$ 2 squares $\frac{1}{4}$ 3 squares $\frac{1}{3}$ 4 squares

$\frac{5}{12}$ 5 squares $\frac{1}{2}$ 6 squares $\frac{7}{12}$ 7 squares $\frac{2}{3}$ 8 squares

$\frac{3}{4}$ 9 squares $\frac{5}{6}$ 10 squares $\frac{11}{12}$ 11 squares

Use your fraction strips to see what is happening in question 1.71 (i), (ii), (iv), and question 1.72 (i), (ii), (iv).

Make up your own addition and subtraction questions using your fraction strips.

1.73 Setting out your work clearly, to show what you are doing, carry out the following multiplications, leaving your answers in the simplest form.

(i) $\frac{1}{2} \times \frac{1}{3}$ (1)

(ii) $\frac{1}{3} \times \frac{3}{4}$ (1)

(iii) $\frac{1}{2} \times \frac{3}{5}$ (1)

(iv) $\frac{3}{4} \times \frac{5}{6}$ (1)

(v) $\frac{7}{8} \times \frac{4}{7}$ (1)

(vi) $1\frac{1}{2} \times \frac{3}{4}$ (1)

1.74 Setting out your work clearly, to show what you are doing, carry out the following divisions.

(i) $\frac{1}{2} \div \frac{1}{3}$ (1)

(ii) $\frac{1}{3} \div \frac{3}{4}$ (1)

(iii) $\frac{1}{2} \div \frac{3}{5}$ (1)

(iv) $\frac{1}{4} \div \frac{1}{6}$ (1)

(v) $\frac{7}{8} \div \frac{3}{16}$ (1)

(vi) $1\frac{1}{2} \div \frac{2}{3}$ (1)

1.75 (a)   You will need a copy of the number line below.

On your copy, mark with crosses and label clearly

(i)   1.3 (1)

(ii) 1.75 (1)

(iii) 1.05 (1)

(b)   Which decimal is exactly halfway between

(i)   1.4 and 1.8 (1)

(ii) 1.2 and 1.9 (1)

(iii) 1.5 and 1.85? (1)

1.76 Change

    (i) $\frac{3}{5}$ to a decimal   (1)

    (ii)   0.7 to a fraction   (1)

    (iii) 0.4 to a percentage   (1)

    (iv) 5% to a decimal   (1)

    (v) $\frac{4}{5}$ to a percentage   (1)

    (vi) 45% to a fraction in its simplest form.   (1)

1.77 (a)   You will need three copies of the percentage scale below.

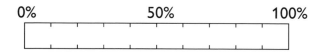

On your copies, shade and label

    (i)   70%   (1)

    (ii)   35%   (1)

    (iii) 5%   (1)

 (b)   A percentage scale is shown below.

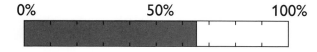

    (i)   What percentage has been shaded?   (1)

    (ii)   What is this written as a decimal?   (1)

    (iii) What is this written as a fraction in its simplest form?   (1)

1.78 (a)   Garry's marks in some tests are shown below.

    maths $\frac{87}{100}$ French 82%   English $\frac{43}{50}$ science 84%   history $\frac{17}{20}$

    What percentage did Garry score in

    (i)   English   (1)

    (ii)   history   (1)

    (iii) the subject with his best score?   (1)

 (b)   The table below shows Sophie's marks in some tests.

Subject	Mark	Percentage
English	$\frac{83}{100}$	83%
maths	$\frac{37}{50}$	
science	$\frac{17}{25}$	
Spanish	$\frac{28}{40}$	

    Copy and complete the table by recording the percentages.   (3)

1.79 500 people took part in a survey carried out by a clothing company to help them choose their colour range for the next season.

Some of the results are shown in the table below.

Selected colour	Number of people	Popularity position
red		
blue	9	
green		
yellow		
purple	375	1st
pink		

Copy and complete the table, using the clues below. (6)

- 5% of those surveyed chose red.
- Ten people chose pink.
- One more person selected green than selected yellow.

1.80 (a) At the cinema, 65% of the audience was female.

(i) What percentage of the audience was male? (1)

Altogether, 200 people watched the film.

(ii) How many males were in the audience? (2)

(b) In a box of 72 sweets, 25% are mints.

(i) How many mints are there? (1)

A third of the sweets are chocolates and the rest are toffees.

(ii) How many toffees are there? (2)

1.81 During the sales, the prices of identical mobile phones are reduced at four shops as shown in the table below.

Shop	Usual price	Sale bargain	New price
A	£115	20% off	
B	£124	reduced by $\frac{1}{4}$	
C	£135	$\frac{1}{3}$ off all phones	
D	£140	30% off	£98

Copy and complete the table to show which shop is offering the best deal. (6)

1.82 (a) A bag contains 40 balls. 20% of the balls are red, $\frac{1}{8}$ of the balls are blue and three of the balls are yellow. The rest of the balls are green.

     (i)   How many balls are red?   (1)

     (ii)   How many balls are blue?   (1)

     (iii)   How many balls are green?   (1)

(b) The ingredients in a new chocolate bar, weighing 96 grams, are shown on the label below.

> 24 g fudge
> 22 g raisins
> 16 g nuts
> 8 g wafer

The rest of the bar is chocolate.

     (i)   What is the mass of chocolate?   (1)

     (ii)   What fraction, in its simplest form, of the total mass is fudge?   (1)

     (iii)   What is the mass of fudge as a percentage of the total mass of the ingredients? (1)

1.83 (a) Hens' eggs contain 78% water and 10% fat. The remainder is protein.

     (i)   What percentage of an egg is protein?   (1)

     (ii)   What fraction, in its simplest form, of an egg is water?   (1)

(b) Every 100 g of skimmed milk contains the following nutrients.

> | | |
> |---|---|
> | fat | 2 g |
> | protein | 36 g |
> | carbohydrate | 52 g |
> | water | 10 g |

     (i)   What fraction of skimmed milk is protein?   (1)

     (ii)   What percentage of skimmed milk is fat?   (1)

Celia drinks a glass of milk containing 250 g of skimmed milk.

     (iii)   What percentage of the milk Celia drinks is fat?   (1)

     (iv)   What is the mass of the fat in the glass of milk?   (1)

Challenge 1K

Study the nutrition labels from food packets. Work out the fractions and percentages of fat, carbohydrate and protein in each food. You may get a few surprises!

You could compare the nutrition of chocolate bars or packets of crisps. This is a mathematical study so it isn't necessary to eat all the contents!

1.84 Colin asked each of the 400 boys in the school to name his favourite team sport. The results are shown in the table.

Favourite sport	Number of boys
rugby	160
soccer	120
hockey	80
basketball	40

Colin has decided to work out the fraction and percentage of boys who like each sport best. He has made a start. Copy and complete the table below. (6)

Favourite sport	Fraction of boys	Percentage of boys
rugby	$\frac{160}{400} = \frac{2}{5}$	40%
soccer		
hockey		
basketball		

1.85 Copy and complete the table below, which shows equivalent fractions, decimals and percentages. (6)

Fraction in simplest form	$\frac{1}{5}$	$\frac{3}{4}$			$\frac{3}{10}$
Decimal		0.75		0.1	0.3
Percentage	20%		65%		30%

1.86 The drawing shows woodlice in a choice chamber.

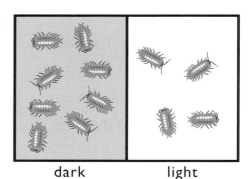

dark   light

(i)   How many woodlice are in the light side? (1)

(ii)   What fraction of the woodlice are in the dark side? (1)

What is the ratio of the number of woodlice in the light to

(iii)   the number of woodlice in the dark (1)

(iv)   the total number of woodlice? (1)

One woodlouse moves from the light into the dark.

What is the new ratio of the number of woodlice in the light to

(v)   the number of woodlice in the dark (1)

(vi)   the total number of woodlice? (1)

1.87 The block graph below shows the numbers of boys and girls in a class.

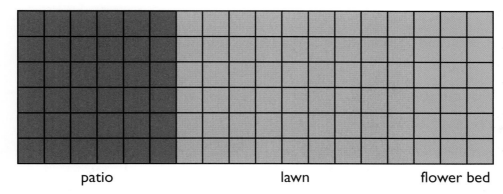

boys

girls

Key: ☐ represents 1 child.

What is the ratio of the numbers of

(i)   boys to girls   (1)

(ii)   girls to boys   (1)

(iii)   girls to the total number of pupils in the class   (1)

(iv)   girls to boys to the number in the whole class?   (1)

One girl leaves the class.

(v)   What is the new ratio of the numbers of boys to girls to the whole class, in its simplest form?   (2)

1.88 This drawing shows Chiara's garden, which is 18 m long and 6 m wide.

patio   lawn   flower bed

Give all answers in their simplest form (lowest terms).

What fraction of the garden is

(i)   patio   (1)

(ii)   lawn?   (1)

Write down the ratio

(iii)   area of patio : area of flower bed   (1)

(iv)   area of lawn : area of whole garden   (1)

(v)   area of patio : area of lawn   (1)

(vi)   area of patio : area of lawn : area of flower bed.   (1)

1.89 (a)   Alexandra's cats, Cookie, Biscuit and Shortbread, find a packet of 20 cat treats.

Cookie and Biscuit eat four treats each and Shortbread eats half of the remainder.

(i)   How many treats does Shortbread eat?   (1)

(ii)   What is the ratio of the numbers of biscuits eaten by Cookie, Biscuit and Shortbread?   (1)

(b)   Jo is reading a book which has 540 pages. So far, Jo has read 90 pages.

(i)   What is the ratio, in its simplest form, of the numbers of

pages Jo has read : pages still to be read?   (1)

Jo reads another third of the book.

(ii)   How many pages has Jo now read altogether?   (1)

(iii)   What is the new ratio, in its simplest form, of the numbers of

pages Jo has read : pages still to be read?   (1)

Jo reads more of the book and reaches page 450 before she falls asleep.

(iv)   What is the new ratio, in its simplest form, of the numbers of

pages Jo has read : pages still to be read?   (1)

1.90 Annabel, Brian and Clarissa share all the sweets from a bag in the ratio

3 : 2 : 4

(i)   What can you say about the number of sweets in the bag?   (1)

Clarissa receives 12 sweets.

(ii)   How many sweets are received by

(a)   Brian   (1)

(b)   Annabel?   (1)

(iii)   How many sweets were in the unopened bag?   (1)

Annabel eats a third of her sweets and Brian and Clarissa each eat half of theirs.

(iv)   What is the ratio, in its simplest form, of the numbers of sweets that Annabel, Brian and Clarissa now have?   (2)

1.91 (a)   The angles of a triangle are in the ratio 1 : 4 : 4

(i)   What is the smallest angle of the triangle?   (1)

(ii)   What type of triangle is this?   (1)

(b)   Mary's recipe to make 12 chocolate buns uses 80 grams of chocolate.

(i)   What mass of chocolate would be needed to make 24 buns?   (1)

(ii)   How many buns could be made if Mary has only 120 grams of chocolate?   (1)

(c)   When making concrete, Angus mixes cement, sand and gravel in the ratio 1 : 2 : 3

Angus calculates that he needs about nine buckets of concrete and he measures the quantities using a bucket. How many buckets full of each material will Angus put into the mix?   (2)

2 CALCULATIONS

2.1 NUMBER OPERATIONS

Questions involving

- the four basic operations
- making use of number facts
- the order of operations

Calculation skills feature in many questions throughout this book.

2.01 You may have seen a diagram like the one below, with 'jumps' on a number line, showing an addition fact.

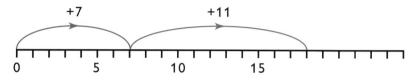

In this case, the diagram shows the addition fact 7 + 11 = 18

(i) The diagram below shows the same addition fact, 7 + 11 = 18

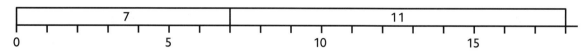

On a copy of the number line, represent the addition fact 5 + 8 = … in the same way. (1)

(ii) The diagram below shows the subtraction fact 13 − 9 = 4

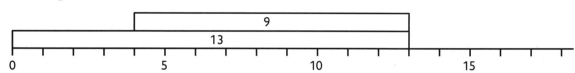

On a copy of the number line, represent the subtraction fact 14 − 9 = … (1)

(iii) The diagram below shows the multiplication fact 6 × 3 = 18

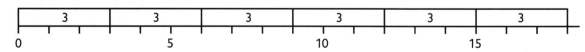

On a copy of the number line, represent the multiplication fact 5 × 4 = … (1)

(iv) The diagram below shows the exact division fact 16 ÷ 4 = 4

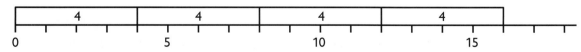

On a copy of the number line, represent the division fact 21 ÷ 3 = … (1)

(v) The diagram below shows the non-exact division fact 16 ÷ 3 = 5 remainder 1

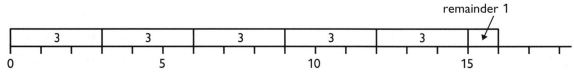

On a copy of the number line, represent the non-exact division fact 23 ÷ 5 = … (1)

(vi) The diagram below shows the subtraction fact $8 - 11 = {}^-3$

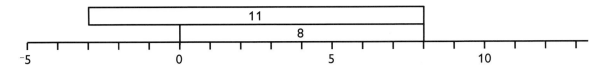

On a copy of the number line, represent the subtraction fact $11 - 13 = \dots$ (1)

2.02 Write down

(i) the sum of 18 and 27 (1)

(ii) the difference between 40 and 31 (1)

(iii) the product of 9 and 6 (1)

Write down the result, stating the remainder where appropriate, when 28 is divided by

(iv) 4 (1)

(v) 5 (1)

(vi) 6 (1)

2.03 Write down

(i) the sum of 43, 18 and 131 (1)

(ii) the difference between 62 and 37 (1)

(iii) the product of 13 and 7 (1)

Write down the result, stating the remainder where appropriate, when 60 is divided by

(iv) 5 (1)

(v) 8 (1)

(vi) 7 (1)

2.04 (a) Graham has three lengths of wood: 15 cm, 33 cm and 29 cm. If the lengths are placed end to end, how far will they stretch? (1)

(b) Iain has 132 stamps and Sally has 87 stamps. How many more stamps than Sally does Iain have? (1)

(c) If the difference between two numbers is 23 and the larger number is 61, what is the smaller number? (1)

(d) The masses of four parcels are 2.3 kg, 0.9 kg, 1.6 kg and 0.7 kg. What is the total mass of the parcels? (1)

(e) Pallab has grown 7.5 cm since his last birthday. His height is now 154.5 cm. What was his height last birthday? (1)

(f) At the start of the day, Amanda's pencil measured 11.7 cm. By the end of the day the pencil was half as long. How long was the pencil at the end of the day? (1)

2.05 Copy the following and write in the missing numbers.

    (i) $37 + \underline{\hspace{1cm}} = 72$ (1)

    (ii) $7 + 45 + \underline{\hspace{1cm}} = 83$ (1)

    (iii) $18 + 62 - 33 = \underline{\hspace{1cm}}$ (1)

    (iv) $102 - \underline{\hspace{1cm}} = 89$ (1)

    (v) $13 \times \underline{\hspace{1cm}} = 52$ (1)

    (vi) $54 \div \underline{\hspace{1cm}} = 6$ (1)

2.06 (a)   A known addition fact is $17 + 11 = 28$

           Using the same numbers 11, 17 and 28 in each fact, write down the other addition fact and the two associated subtraction facts.   (3)

     (b)   A known multiplication fact is $18 \times 3 = 54$

           Using the same numbers 3, 18 and 54 in each fact, write down the other multiplication fact and the two associated division facts.   (3)

2.07 A known number fact is $5 + 7 = 12$

Use this fact to help you to calculate

    (i) $50 + 70 = \underline{\hspace{1cm}}$ (1)

    (iii) $0.5 + 0.7 = \underline{\hspace{1cm}}$ (1)

    (iii) $1200 - \underline{\hspace{1cm}} = 500$ (1)

    (iv)   Why could this number fact *not* be used to help you calculate $5 + 70$?   (1)

Taking great care, calculate

    (v) $0.5 + 7 = \underline{\hspace{1cm}}$ (1)

    (vi) $1200 - 50 = \underline{\hspace{1cm}}$ (1)

2.08 A known number fact is $5 \times 7 = 35$

Use this fact to help you to calculate

    (i) $50 \times 7 = \underline{\hspace{1cm}}$ (1)

    (ii) $50 \times 0.7 = \underline{\hspace{1cm}}$ (1)

    (iii) $0.5 \times 0.7 = \underline{\hspace{1cm}}$ (1)

    (iv) $35 \div 0.7 = \underline{\hspace{1cm}}$ (1)

    (v) $3.5 \div 0.7 = \underline{\hspace{1cm}}$ (1)

    (vi) $35 \div 70 = \underline{\hspace{1cm}}$ (1)

2.09 Taking great care over the order of operations, calculate

    (i) $5 + 4 \times 6 =$ _____   (1)

    (ii) $(5 + 4) \times 6 =$ _____   (1)

    (iii) $12 - 8 + 4 \times 2 =$ _____   (1)

    (iv) $(10 - 3) + 5 \times 4 - 8 =$ _____   (1)

    (v) $16 - 3 \times 5 + 4 \div 2 =$ _____   (1)

    (vi) $(3^2 + 2 \times 5 - 4) \times 2 =$ _____   (1)

2.10 Amelia has the three digit cards and four operation cards shown below.

She combines the three digit cards using two operation cards, for example as shown below.

In the example, the result is 28

How could she arrange the cards to give the result

    (i)   20   (1)

    (ii)   35   (1)

    (iii)   4?   (1)

Amelia adds a pair of bracket cards **(** and **)** so she can get different results, for example as shown below.

In this example, the result is 36

How could Amelia arrange her cards, using the brackets if necessary, to give the result

    (iv) 44   (1)

    (v)   ⁻1   (1)

    (vi) 6?   (1)

2.11 As quickly as possible, complete a copy of the addition grid below. (6)

+	4	9	6	3	8	5	7
8							
3							
7							
4							
6							
9							
5							

2.12 As quickly as possible, complete a copy of the multiplication grid below. (6)

×	4	9	6	3	8	5	7
8							
3							
7							
4							
6							
9							
5							

2.13 As quickly as possible, complete a copy of the subtraction grid below, recording a negative number if necessary. (6)

−	4	3	7	6	5
5		2			
6					
8					
7					
9		2			

2.14 Write the answers to the following divisions, recording a remainder where appropriate.

   (i) $15 \div 4$ (1)

   (ii) $19 \div 5$ (1)

   (iii) $43 \div 3$ (1)

   (iv) $42 \div 7$ (1)

   (v) $34 \div 6$ (1)

   (vi) $105 \div 48$ (1)

2.2 MENTAL STRATEGIES

Questions involving

● **a wide variety of strategies, including using a step-by-step approach**
● **checking**

For all questions in this section you should do no written working, but simply write the answers. Do all the questions in your head and check that each answer is sensible.

2.15 Calculate

(i)	$16 + 35$	(1)
(ii)	$50 - 29$	(1)
(iii)	49×5	(1)
(iv)	$11 + 17 + 19 + 23$	(1)
(v)	5×16	(1)
(vi)	13^2	(1)

2.16 Calculate

(i)	$71 + 49$	(1)
(ii)	$200 - 59$	(1)
(iii)	99×8	(1)
(iv)	$37 + 13 + 62 + 38$	(1)
(v)	15×24	(1)
(vi)	21^2	(1)

2.17 Calculate

(i)	$\frac{5}{8}$ of $64\,$kg	(1)
(ii)	15% of £400	(1)
(iii)	0.4×7	(1)
(iv)	$185 \div 5$	(1)
(v)	$9 \times £9.99$	(1)
(vi)	$204 \div 12$	(1)

2.18 (a) What is the cost of nine chocolate bars costing 49 pence each? (1)

(b) How many people could each get a third of a pizza if there are only five pizzas left? (1)

(c) The temperature inside Dr Foster's car was $16\,°$C but the temperature outside was 19 degrees lower. What was the temperature outside the car? (1)

(d) A film on TV started at 19:55 and ended at 22:05

How long was the film? (1)

(e) The product of two integers between 2 and 10 inclusive is 45

What is the sum of the integers? (1)

(f) The sum of two different prime numbers is 14

What is the product of the two prime numbers? (1)

2.19 Calculate

    (i)   35% of \$600   (1)

    (ii) 0.05×0.2 (1)

    (iii) $19 \times £12.01$ (1)

    (iv) $414 \div 18$ (1)

    (v) $\frac{2}{3}$ of 48 litres   (1)

    (vi) 2030×5 (1)

2.3 WRITTEN METHODS

Questions involving

● **addition**
● **subtraction**
● **multiplication, including long multiplication**
● **division, including division using factors**

For all the questions in this section you are expected to set out full working clearly, even if you could do the calculations in your head.

2.20 (a)   Add 239 to 108   (1)

      (b)   Subtract 489 from 1040   (1)

      (c)   Multiply 37 by 73   (2)

      (d)   Divide 861 by 7   (2)

2.21 (a)   Add 47.5 to 16.9   (1)

      (b)   Subtract 19.8 from 41.3   (1)

      (c)   Multiply 7.2 by 1.8   (2)

      (d)   Divide 132.3 by 9   (2)

2.22 (a)   Add 40.9 to 4.09   (1)

      (b)   Subtract 4.09 from 40.9   (1)

      (c)   Multiply 7.6 by 1.5   (2)

      (d)   Divide 42.4 by 0.8   (2)

2.23 (a)   Add 0.405 to 0.596   (1)

      (b)   Subtract 6.78 from 8.6   (1)

      (c)   Multiply 0.95 by 1.3   (2)

      (d)   Divide 1.08 by 0.6   (2)

2.24 (a)   Which number is 7.8 less than 13.05?   (1)

      (b)   What must be added to 27.4 to get 103.15?   (1)

      (c)   What is the difference between 14.3 and ⁻6.7?   (1)

      (d)   Divide 14.5 by 5   (1)

      (e)   What is the product of 17.3 and 4.9?   (2)

2.25 (a) What is the cost of 13 chocolate bars which are priced at 57 pence each? (2)

(b) 11 people share a lottery prize of £27 380

How much will each person receive, to the nearest pound? (2)

(c) A field measures 116 metres by 59 metres. What is the area of the field? (2)

2.4 CALCULATOR METHODS

Questions involving

● interpreting calculator displays

For the questions in this section you should *not* use a calculator!

2.26 (a) Charlie multiplied 45 by 72 using her calculator and wrote down the answer 3195

Why should Charlie have realised straight away that she had made a mistake? (1)

(b) Brendan divided 400 by 39 using his calculator and wrote down the answer 10.256 410 26

He did a quick mental calculation to check.

(i) Suggest what his mental calculation was. (1)

(ii) Write Brendan's calculator result correct to 3 significant figures. (1)

(c) Nicole has tried to do the calculation 36.76 + 1.17 using her calculator.

Her calculator display shows the following result.

$$35.59$$

Nicole realises that this cannot be correct.

(i) Suggest two reasons why Nicole knows that the result is incorrect. (2)

(ii) Suggest what might have gone wrong. (1)

2.27 Jon used his calculator to perform a calculation. The display is shown below.

$$5.25$$

Interpret this calculator display in more appropriate ways, given the clues.

(i) time (in hours and minutes) (1)

(ii) number of pizzas to be purchased if 21 people each want a quarter of a pizza (1)

(iii) cost of a meal (in pounds) (1)

(iv) addition of the fractions $3\frac{3}{4}$ and $1\frac{1}{2}$ (1)

(v) mass (in stones and pounds) (1)

(vi) the number of people Jon can afford to invite to his birthday party (1)

2.28 Write each of these calculator answers as a whole number, a proper fraction or a mixed number.

(i) 3.5 (1)

(ii) 4.75 (1)

(iii) 8.125 (1)

(iv) 4.666666667 (1)

(v) 9.999999999 (1)

(vi) 0.555555555 (1)

2.29 (a) Sandra divided 1428 by 6 using her calculator. The calculator gave the result as 285.6

Sandra knew, before doing the calculation, that the answer should be an integer (whole number).

(i) Why did she know that the correct answer is an integer? (1)

(ii) What should the answer be? (1)

(iii) What error do you think Sandra made? (1)

(b) Kasia performed a calculation using her calculator. The display is shown below.

$$6.666666667$$

Write the result in a more appropriate form given the information.

(i) time (in minutes and seconds) (1)

(ii) height (in feet and inches) (1)

(iii) distance (in yards and feet) (1)

2.30 (a) Lewis thought of a number, added 7 and then multiplied by 5

In his head, he calculated that the result was 50

(i) What number did Lewis think of? (1)

Using his calculator to check, Lewis was surprised to get the result 38

(ii) Suggest two ways that Lewis could have made sure that his calculator result was correct. (2)

(b) Andrea did a correct pencil and paper addition to find the sum of 14.5 and 36.4

(i) What result did Andrea get? (1)

She then used her calculator to check and, to her surprise, got 181.4, which she knew could not be correct!

(ii) What mistake did Andrea make when using the calculator? (1)

Andrea used her calculator a second time and, to her disbelief, got yet another answer, 50.5

(iii) What mistake did Andrea make this time? (1)

2.5 CHECKING RESULTS

Questions involving

- **strategies which can be used**

2.31 The following calculations have all been done *incorrectly*. For each one, say what the correct answer should be.

    (i) $45 - 18 = 33$ (1)

    (ii) $117 + 29 = 136$ (1)

    (iii) $14 \times 6 = 74$ (1)

    (iv) $180 \div 12 = 16$ (1)

    (v) $13 - 8 \times 4 = 20$ (1)

    (vi) $(8 + 12) \div 4 = 11$ (1)

2.32 (a) Taylor multiplied 24 by 0.75 and wrote the result incorrectly as 16

        Do the equivalent calculation of dividing 24 by 4 and then multiplying by 3 $\left(\text{in other words, multiplying by } \frac{3}{4}\right)$ to find the correct result.   (2)

    (b) Sean multiplied 19.7 by 3.9 and wrote the result incorrectly as 768.3

        What should the result be?   (2)

    (c) When Andrea thought of a number, multiplied by 8 and then subtracted 17, she got 39

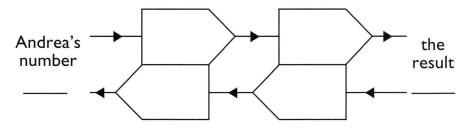

    On a copy of the flowchart above, fill in the information given and then 'work backwards' using the inverse operations to find Andrea's number.   (2)

2.33 Copy and complete the following statements.

    (i)   An integer ending in 5 plus an integer ending in 8 always gives an integer ending in ____   (1)

    (ii)   An integer ending in 5 minus an integer ending in 8 always gives an integer ending in ____   (1)

    (iii)   An integer ending in 5 times an integer ending in 8 always gives an integer ending in ____   (1)

    (iv)   An integer ending in 7 plus an integer ending in ____ always gives an integer ending in 1   (1)

    (v)   An integer ending in 7 minus an integer ending in ____ always gives an integer ending in 9   (1)

    (vi)   An integer ending in 7 plus an integer ending in ____ always gives an integer ending in 9   (1)

2.34 If you are working very quickly, or not concentrating, you can sometimes misread a question.

In each of the following examples, the answer is incorrect. For each one, say what the correct answer should be and suggest why the mistake was made.

(i)   Add 3 to $^-4$

     Incorrect answer given: 7   (2)

(ii)   List the positive integers, i, which satisfy the inequality $i \leqslant 5$

     Incomplete answer given: 1, 2, 3, 4   (2)

(iii) List the numbers between 10 and 20, inclusive, which are not multiples of 3

     Incorrect answer given: 12, 15, 18   (2)

Challenge 2A

It would be a good idea to study all questions on which you gained less than full marks and see how many extra marks you might have gained if you had checked your answers carefully. We all make mistakes!

Challenge 2B

Using a set of number cards 1 to 9, take 4 cards at random to make two 2-digit numbers. For example:

For the two numbers, e.g. 53 and 69, write down the units digit and an estimate, to 1 significant figure, of the size of:

(i)   the sum of the numbers

(ii)   the difference between the numbers

(iii) the product of the numbers.

In this example, we have:

(i)   2,   100

(ii)   6,   20

(iii) 7,   4000

You could challenge your friends to a competition and invent a points scoring system.

3 PROBLEM SOLVING

3.1 DECISION MAKING

Questions involving

- understanding the problem
- deciding on a suitable strategy

3.01 Consider the four basic operations:

        adding   **subtracting**   **multiplying**   **dividing**

and the operations:

        squaring   **finding a square root**

Write down the operation or combination of operations which you might use to find a solution to each of the following problems.

Write the operation or operations in order. You do not need to find the solution.

(i)   Six people share £450 equally. How much will each person receive?   (1)

(ii)   A rectangular field measures 65 m by 105 m. What is the area of the field?   (1)

(iii) Tom had 48 marbles. He lost 29 to James and then won 27 from Bill.

      How many marbles does Tom have now?   (1)

(iv) Hamish has 5 sweets, Flora has 7 sweets and Maggie has 18 sweets.

      They put all their sweets in a bag and then share them equally. How many sweets will each receive?   (1)

(v)   Sarah arranges some 2p coins in six rows of six piles of ten coins.

      What is the total value, in pounds, of the coins?   (1)

(vi) A square has area 64 m². What is perimeter of the square?   (1)

3.02 Find the solution to each of the problems in question 3.01   (6)

3.03 Consider the general methods:

     mental (M)   **mental with jottings (MJ)**   **pencil and paper (PP)**
           practical (PR)   **calculator (C)**

Decide which method or methods you would choose in order to solve each of the following problems.

Write the method or methods in order. You do not need to find the solution.

(i)   How many 1p coins in a straight line would stretch 1 m?   (1)

(ii)   What is the cost of ten chocolate bars priced at 59 pence each?   (1)

(iii) What is the cube root of 500?   (1)

(iv) What is 532 divided by 14?   (1)

(v)   What is the perimeter of a rectangle measuring 13.7 cm by 4.6 cm?   (1)

(vi) How many 1p coins could be placed around a single 2p coin, just touching it?   (1)

Each of the next five questions makes use of one of the most useful strategies in problem solving. In each question, show and/or explain clearly how you are tackling the problem.

3.04 Making an organised list

List, in order of increasing size, all of the two-digit and three-digit numbers which can be made using the three digit cards shown below. (6)

3.05 Trying a practical approach

The diagram below shows a regular hexagon with its diagonals drawn.

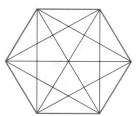

If a regular hexagon has all of its diagonals drawn, how many, and what, shapes are between the diagonals? (6)

> **Challenge 3A**
>
> Using the ideas in question 3.05, you might like to carry out an investigation into the numbers and types of shapes between the diagonals of other regular shapes, for example regular pentagons or octagons.

3.06 Guessing and checking

(a) The sum of two prime numbers, each less than 40, is 50 and their product is 481

What are the two primes? (2)

(b) The product of two primes, between 40 and 70, is 2867 and the difference between them is 14

What are the two primes? (4)

3.07 Trying something simpler

The diagram below shows a step pyramid made up of three layers of small cubes.

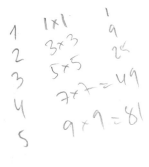

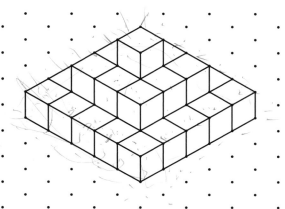

How many small cubes will be needed to build a step pyramid with five layers? (6)

Looking for a pattern

The diagram below shows the first three patterns in a sequence made from drinking straws.

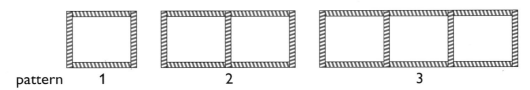

pattern   1   2   3

Pattern 1 uses 4 straws, pattern 2 uses 7 straws, and so on.

How many straws would be needed for pattern number 10?   (6)

3.2 REASONING ABOUT NUMBERS OR SHAPES

Questions involving

- **number or shape puzzles**
- **looking for patterns**
- **making general statements**

Throughout this section, keep in mind the ideas covered in section 3.1 and ask yourself questions such as 'What if …?', 'What happens when …?', 'How …?'

3.09 William and Mary have each thought of a single-digit positive integer larger than 1

When they add the two numbers, the result is an odd number.

(i)   Is the difference between their numbers odd or even?   (1)

(ii)   Is the product of their numbers odd or even?   (1)

(iii)   If William's number divides exactly by Mary's number, is the result odd or even?   (1)

(iv)   Is the square of William's number odd or even?   (1)

(v)   What numbers have William and Mary thought of?   (1)

(vi)   What is the result of dividing Mary's number by William's number?   (1)

3.10 (a)   The sum of two numbers is 47, and one number is 31 smaller than the other.

(i)   What are the two numbers?   (1)

(ii)   What is the product of the two numbers?   (1)

(b)   Two prime numbers have a product of 65

For these two primes, what is

(i)   the smaller   (1)

(ii)   the sum?   (1)

(c)   The mean (average) of three prime numbers, all with the same units digit and each less than 30, is 13

What are the prime numbers?   (2)

3.11 (a)   Three integers have a product of 70 and a sum of 14

What are the integers?   (2)

(b)   Which two integers have a product of 303 and a sum of 104?   (2)

(c)   Which is the smallest number that can be divided by both 24 and 40?   (2)

3.12 (a)   When Amy thought of a number, multiplied it by 4 and then subtracted 5, she got the result 23

What number did Amy think of?   (1)

(b)   When Barbara thought of a number, subtracted 5 and then multiplied by 4, she got the result 8

What number did Barbara think of?   (1)

(c)   When Charles thought of a positive integer, squared it and then added his original number, the result was 20

What number did Charles think of?   (2)

(d)   When Donna thought of a number, multiplied it by 3 and then subtracted 12, the result was the number she thought of!

What number did Donna think of?   (2)

3.13 (a)   Elle is thinking of a number and has given these clues.

The number is

● a multiple of 3

● between 5 and 20

● 1 less than a square number.

What is Elle's number?   (2)

(b)   Fred is thinking of a plane shape and has given these clues.

The shape has

● four sides

● one, and only one, line of symmetry.

Name at least two possible shapes that Fred could be thinking of.   (2)

(c)   Gill is thinking of a number and has given these clues.

The number is

● smaller than 50

● 2 more than a multiple of 6

● 1 less than a multiple of 5

Write down two possibilities for Gill's number.   (2)

3.14 (a) Hassan is thinking of a solid shape and has given these clues.

The shape has

- five faces

- eight edges of equal length.

What shape is Hassan thinking of? (2)

(b) Isla is thinking of a number and has given these clues.

The number has

- three digits with a sum of 6

- the prime factors 2, 3 and 11

What number is Isla thinking of? (2)

(c) Jenny is thinking of a plane shape and has given these clues.

The shape has

- fewer than eight sides

- two, and only two, lines of symmetry

- no right angles.

Name two possibilities for Jenny's shape. (2)

3.15 The integers 6 and 9 have a difference of **3**

They have a sum of **15**

The difference between their squares (81 − 36) is **45**

Notice that **3 × 15 = 45**

(i) 4 and 7 also have a difference of 3

They have a sum of 11

Write down the difference between their squares (49 − 16) (1)

(ii) Write down the multiplication fact like the one in the example. (1)

(iii) Repeat the procedure for your own choice of a pair of integers with a difference of 3, and say what you notice. (2)

(iv) Without squaring either number, what will be the difference between the squares of 19 and 22? (2)

Challenge 3B

Using the ideas in question 3.15, you might like to carry out an investigation where the two integers have a difference of 5 – or any other difference! See what you can discover.

The following example might help you to amaze your friends and parents!

4 and 5 have a difference of 1 and a sum of 9

The difference between their squares is 9 (25 − 16).

Without doing any squaring, you should be able to say confidently that the difference between the squares of 2000 and 2001 is 4001 (1 × the sum of the numbers). In the same way, the difference between the squares of 12 and 13 is 25

3.16 (a) Gail has five different coins, with a total value of 68 pence, in her purse.

(i) What are the five coins? (1)

Gail buys an ice-cream costing 53 pence. She hands over two of her coins and receives three coins in change.

(ii) Which coins does she hand over? (1)

(iii) Which three coins does she receive in change? (1)

(b) Roger and Pat give equal amounts of their pocket money to Jason who has lost all his money. Roger gives Jason exactly a third of his money and Pat gives Jason exactly a quarter of his money. Jason now has £4.00

(i) How much did Roger have originally? (1)

(ii) How much did Pat have originally? (1)

(iii) How much more does Pat have now than Roger? (1)

3.17 Sakina has drawn the two shapes below, each made up of eight small squares.

(i) What is the order of rotational symmetry of shape A? (1)

(ii) How many lines of symmetry has shape B? (1)

On squared paper, draw and label the following shapes made up of eight squares.

(iii) Shape C, which has rotational symmetry of order 2 but no line symmetry (1)

(iv) Shape D, which has rotational symmetry of order 4 but no line symmetry (1)

(v) Shape E, which has rotational symmetry of order 4 and four lines of symmetry (2)

Challenge 3C

Using the ideas in question 3.17, see how many different shapes you can make with eight squares, and investigate their symmetries.

Using the same ideas, investigate the shapes *with symmetry* that can be made using 9 squares. What is it about 9 squares that can make the shapes interesting?

3.18 Alexander has the five digit cards shown here.

$$2 \quad 9 \quad 5 \quad 8 \quad 3$$

Arrange any number of the cards to make

  (i)   the largest even number (1)

  (ii)   the largest two-digit prime number (1)

  (iii)   the largest four-digit multiple of 3 (1)

  (iv)   the largest multiple of 5 (1)

  (v)   the smallest number with a digit sum of 11 (1)

  (vi)   the smallest three-digit multiple of 6 (1)

3.19 Applying a rule, over and over again, to a number can be interesting. For example, if we follow the rule *'multiply the sum of the digits by 3'* to 23, we get the result

$$23 \rightarrow 15 \rightarrow 18 \rightarrow \mathbf{27} \rightarrow 27 \rightarrow 27$$

The sequence starts to repeat when it reaches 27

Setting your work out as in the example above, apply the same rule to the following numbers.

  (i)   56 (1)

  (ii)   64 (1)

  (iii)   21 (1)

  (iv)   Find a number between 50 and 60 which starts to repeat after just one step. (1)

  (v)   What is the smallest number greater than 1000 which will start to repeat after just one step? (1)

  (vi)   What is the largest number less than 1000 which will start to repeat after just one step? (1)

Challenge 3D

You might like to investigate this idea. For example, you could see what would happen if you changed the rule to *'multiply the sum of the digits by 4'*.

The possibilities are endless.

If you have a few odd moments, you could invent a different type of rule such as: 'Starting with a 2-digit number add the product of the digits to the difference between the digits. Stop when you reach a single digit or the sequence repeats.'

Examples:

23 → 7   (2 × 3 + 1)

54 → 21 → 3

89 → 73 → 25 → 13 → 5

47 → 31 → 5

See what you can discover.

3.20 In the grid below, each number in an orange square is the mean (average) of the numbers on either side of it.

3	7	11
5	9	13
7	11	15

(i) Describe the patterns that you see in the grid above. (2)

(ii) Copy and complete the grid below using the same pattern. (2)

2	4	
5		9

(iii) Copy and complete the grid below using the same pattern. (2)

8	15	
		40

3.21 The number 212 has a digit sum of 5 (2 + 1 + 2).

(i) Complete an ordered list of all of the six numbers below 100 which have a digit sum of 5 (1)

(ii) Complete an ordered list of the numbers between 100 and 200 which have a digit sum of 5 (1)

(iii) Complete an ordered list of the numbers between 200 and 500 which have a digit sum of 5 (2)

(iv) What is the smallest number larger than 500 which has a digit sum of 5? (1)

(v) What is the largest number less than a million which has a digit sum of 5? (1)

Challenge 3E

A palindromic number is one that reads the same backwards and forwards.

Examples:

44, 383, 1001 and 14541 are all palindromic numbers.

List, in order of size, all of the palindromic numbers smaller than one million that have a digit sum of 5

3.22 James has made copies of Sakina's shapes (see question 3.17), each made up of eight small squares.

Both shapes have an area of 8 square units.

(i)   What is the perimeter of shape A? (1)

(ii)   What is the perimeter of shape B? (1)

On centimetre squared paper, draw and label the following shapes made up of eight squares.

(iii)   Shape C, which has a perimeter of 18 cm (1)

(iv)   Shape D, which has a perimeter of 16 cm (1)

(v)   Shape E, which has a perimeter of 14 cm (2)

Challenge 3F

Using the ideas in this question, see how many different shapes you can make with eight squares, and investigate their perimeters.

3.23 Using the number 5 three times, it is possible to make many number sentences. For example

$$5 + 5 + 5 = 15 \qquad \frac{5}{5} + 5 = 6$$

Continuing to use the number 5 three times, write number sentences to make the following numbers.

(i)   5 (1)

(ii)   2 (1)

(iii) 30 (1)

(iv)   20 (1)

(v)   ⁻4 (1)

(vi)   0.2 (1)

3.24 Georgie has decided that all numbers with a digit sum of 7 should be called Georgie numbers.

From the Georgie numbers less than 100, name

(i)   two that are multiples of 5   (1)

(ii)   two that are square numbers   (1)

(iii)   three that are prime numbers.   (1)

How many Georgie numbers are there between

(iv)   300 and 400   (1)

(v)   400 and 500   (1)

(vi)   500 and 1000?   (1)

3.25 A regular hexagon can be cut into various smaller shapes. In the diagram below, the regular hexagon has been cut to form a rectangle and two congruent isosceles triangles.

Make four copies of the blank regular hexagon and on your copies draw lines to show how the hexagon can be cut to form

(i)   an equilateral triangle and three congruent isosceles triangles   (1)

(ii)   a kite and two congruent isosceles triangles   (1)

(iii)   three congruent rhombuses   (2)

(iv)   a rhombus, an isosceles trapezium and an equilateral triangle.   (2)

3.26 We can apply the rule *'double the units digit and then add the tens digit'* over and over again to a two-digit number. For example

$$23 \rightarrow 8$$

$$79 \rightarrow 25 \rightarrow 12 \rightarrow 5$$

We stop when we reach a single-digit number.

Show what happens with the following starting numbers.

(i)   11   (1)

(ii)   15   (1)

(iii)   75   (1)

(iv)   Which starting number between 10 and 20 simply repeats and never reaches a single-digit number?   (1)

(v)   Which starting number between 90 and 99 eventually repeats?   (1)

(vi)   Which starting number between 80 and 89 takes five steps to reach a single-digit number?   (1)

You might like to investigate further. Is five the largest number of steps needed to reach a single-digit number? How many two-digit starting numbers start to repeat, and never reach a single-digit number?

Alternatively, you might like to investigate a different rule, for example *'starting with a two-digit number, add the sum of the digits to the product of the digits, and stop when you get a single-digit number or the sequence starts to repeat'.*

3.27 Zahra has drawn the shapes below by joining two congruent pieces.

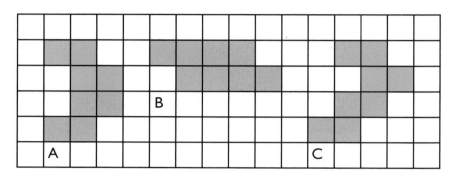

Shape A has reflection symmetry and B has rotation symmetry, but C does not have either reflection or rotation symmetry. Notice how, in shape A, the grey piece has been 'turned over'.

W
13

On squared paper, using the same two congruent pieces, draw

(i)   shape D, a shape with both reflection and rotation symmetry   (2)

(ii)   four different shapes with no symmetry at all.   (4)

You might like to see how many different (non-congruent) shapes you can make by joining these two congruent pieces.

You might also like to investigate the shapes that can be made by joining together two congruent pieces like this:

Don't forget that you can 'turn the piece over'.

3.28 The diagram below shows the first three patterns in a sequence.

The pattern numbers are shown.

W 13

(i)   On squared paper, draw pattern number 4   (1)

(ii)   Copy and complete the table below.   (5)

Pattern number	1	2	3	4	5
Total number of squares	1	5			
Number of squares added to make from previous pattern		4			
Perimeter of shape (units)	4				

Challenge 3J

You might like to make up your own sequence of patterns and complete a similar table of data.

3.3 REAL-LIFE MATHEMATICS

Questions involving

● everyday situations, with numbers in context, such as in money and measures
● the need to use several mathematical skills at the same time

3.29 (a)   Calculate the cost of

(i)   four scarves priced at £5.99 each   (1)

(ii)   five plastic ducks priced at 85 pence each.   (1)

(b)   Calculate how much each person will receive when

(i)   three people share £17.70   (1)

(ii)   two people share a lottery win of £2 362 500   (1)

(c)   Calculate the total mass of

(i)   two parcels weighing 950 g and 1.35 kg   (1)

(ii)   two dogs weighing 28.5 kg and 31.5 kg   (1)

3.30 (a) Calculate how many

    (i)   5p coins you would get for £500   (1)

    (ii)   15 cm long strips of wood you could cut from a 3 m length   (1)

    (iii) minibuses, each with 17 passenger seats, would be needed to transport six football teams of 11 players.   (1)

(b) Calculate how long

    (i)   a film lasts if it starts at 18:55 and ends at 21:10   (1)

    (ii)   it will take Emma to walk 1 km if she walks at 5 km/h   (1)

    (iii) Jack will need to wait for the next bus if the buses run every hour on the half hour and he arrives 6 minutes late for the 09:30 bus.   (1)

3.31 (a) What is the cost of three 'Kilts and Fiddles' hooded sweatshirts priced at £26.95 each?   (1)

(b) Margo has saved £34.50 towards a new mobile phone costing £105.00

How much does she still need?   (1)

(c) Ella has £12.70 and Felipe has £19.45

How much more does Felipe have than Ella?   (1)

(d) Ben buys four ice lollies costing 69 pence each, four packets of crisps costing 48 pence each and a bar of chocolate costing £2.30

How much change will he receive from a £20 note?   (3)

3.32 (a) The nutrition information from a packet of shortbread fingers is shown here.

NUTRITION INFORMATION		
	mass per 100 g	mass per finger
protein	6 g	1.2 g
carbohydrate	63 g	12.6 g
fat	27 g	5.4 g
fibre	3 g	0.6 g
salt etc	1 g	0.2 g

    (i)   What percentage of a shortbread finger is carbohydrate?   (1)

    (ii)   What is the mass of a shortbread finger?   (1)

    (iii) How many shortbread fingers will there be in a 200 g packet?   (1)

(b) Laura wants to bake 18 scones.

She has a recipe which gives the amounts of the ingredients for 2 dozen scones.

To make 2 dozen scones	
butter	220 g
flour	880 g
baking powder	12 tsp
salt	2 tsp
caster sugar	140 g
sultanas	260 g
milk	600 ml
eggs	4

Copy the list of ingredients and write the quantities Laura will need for 18 scones.   (3)

3.33 (a) Shaun has been given a £10 note to buy cards for his fantasy game.

      (i)   How many cards can he buy if individual cards cost 11 pence each?   (1)

      (ii)   How much change will Shaun receive?   (1)

  (b) Janet cut three 90 cm lengths from a 5 m length of string.

      (i)   What length of string remained?   (1)

  Janet then cut the remaining length of string into two equal pieces.

      (ii)   How long was each of these pieces?   (1)

  (c) Contented Towers School has a total of 563 pupils. 295 of the pupils are boys. How many more boys are there than girls?   (2)

3.34 In the annual school duck race, the ducks were dropped from a bridge at noon. The numbers of ducks passing the finish line were recorded in the pictogram below.

Finish time (minutes)	
12:20 to 12:25	
12:25 to 12:30	
12:30 to 12:35	
12:35 to 12:40	
12:40 to 12:45	
12:45 to 12:50	
12:50 to 12:55	
12:55 to 13:00	
13:00 to 13:05	
later than 13:05	

Key: represents 1 duck.

    (i)   How many ducks finished within 30 minutes of the start?   (1)

    (ii)   How many ducks started the race?   (1)

    (iii) After approximately how many minutes had half of the ducks finished?   (2)

    (iv) What fraction of the ducks finished before 12:25?   (2)

3.35 Work out the cost of each of these items from a shopping list.

    (i)   six apples at 38 pence each   (1)

    (ii)   400 g of tomatoes at £2.50 per kilogram   (1)

    (iii) $1\frac{1}{2}$ kg of potatoes at 90 pence per kilogram   (1)

    (iv) 12 eggs at £1.15 for half a dozen   (1)

    (v)   3 litres of milk where a litre bottle costs 95 pence and a 2 litre bottle costs £1.80   (1)

    (vi) 16 oranges at four for £1.05   (1)

3.36 The costs of the same items in Miss Atrick's basic week's shopping trolley, bought at four different supermarkets, are shown in the table below.

Supermarket	A	B	C	D
General groceries	£110.35	£105.95	£108.12	£113.10
Bread, milk, meat	£15.40	£21.10	£17.50	£16.90
Non-food items	£12.45	£14.30	£13.90	£9.98

(i)   What is the total cost of the items at supermarket A?   (1)

(ii)   How much cheaper are the general groceries at supermarket B than supermarket A?   (1)

(iii)   Which supermarket offers the best price on the items other than general groceries?   (2)

(iv)   Miss Atrick normally shops at supermarket B. How much could she save on the whole week's shopping if she bought all the items at supermarket D?   (2)

3.37 (a)   Soniya tipped the coins from her money box onto the table. She was amazed to see that she had one 1p coin, two 2p coins, five 5p coins, ten 10p coins, twenty 20p coins, fifty 50p coins, one £1 coin and two £2 coins.

(i)   How much did she have altogether?   (3)

(ii)   How much more did Soniya need in order to buy a book reader costing £95?   (1)

(b)   Miss Grant runs a shop selling kilts. She buys 12 casual kilts for £49.95 each and sells them all for £69.99 each. How much profit does she make in total?   (2)

3.38 The diagram below shows the seating plan for the school charity concert.

	1	2	3	4	5	6	7	8	9	10	11	12
A												
B												
C			C3									
D												
E												
F												
G												
H												
I												
J												
K												
L												
M												
N												
O												

The seats are identified by the row letter and a number, for example C3, which is marked on the diagram.

The prices of the seats are given in the table.

Seat	Price
	£10
	£5
	£2

(i) Mr Christie booked a block of eight seats: G5–G8 and H5–H8

Why do you think he booked those seats? (1)

(ii) How many seats are there priced at £10? (1)

(iii) How many seats are there priced at £5? (1)

(iv) If all of the tickets are sold, how much money will be raised? (3)

3.39 (a) The Smith family bought a new three-piece suite for £960 from a furniture store.

The next week, the store had a sale and the same suite was reduced in price by 20%.

How much would the family have saved if they had waited and bought the suite in the sale? (2)

(b) The label on a shirt is shown below.

> polyester and cotton mixture
> 67% polyester

What fraction, approximately, of the material is cotton? (2)

(c) James handed over a £10 note to pay for three cups of tea and received a £5 note, a £2 coin, two 20p coins and a 5p coin in change.

How much was each cup of tea? (2)

3.40 Five friends raised money by cleaning cars. The amounts they each raised are recorded in the table.

Name	Amount
Andy	£7.50
Barry	£9.00
Connor	£6.00
Denise	£13.50
Edward	£12.00

(i) What was the total amount of money raised? (2)

The friends all charged the same amount for cleaning a car and Edward cleaned three more cars than Andy.

(ii) How many cars did Edward clean? (2)

(iii) How many cars were cleaned altogether? (2)

3.41 Arthur plans to build a 24-metre fence down the side of his garden using posts and bars.

He has drawn the sketch below to show how the posts and bars will be fitted together.

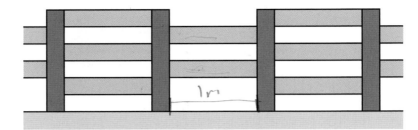

The centres of the fenceposts are 1 metre apart, with rails nailed between them as shown. Arthur starts by placing a post at each end of the side of the garden.

(i) (a) How many posts will he need?   (1)

     (b) How many rails will he need?   (2)

Posts cost £8 each and rails cost £4.50 each.

(ii)   How much will the materials cost?   (2)

The rails are nailed to the posts using two nails at each end.

(iii) How many nails will Arthur use?   (1)

3.42 Four friends decided to see how long they could remain silent. Their times are recorded in the table below.

Name	Time
Keith	1 hour 15 minutes 40 seconds
Lara	1 minute 3 seconds
Max	1 hour 44 minutes 20 seconds
Natascha	58 minutes 57 seconds

(i)   How much longer than Keith did Max remain silent?   (1)

(ii)   What was the mean (average) time that they remained silent?   (2)

Dr Foster offered to give one penny to charity for every second that each of them remained silent.

(iii) How much was raised by

       (a) Lara   (1)

       (b) Max?   (2)

3.43 A classroom is 8 metres long and 6.5 metres wide.

(i)   What is the area of the floor?   (1)

The floor is to be covered in 50 cm square carpet tiles.

(ii)   How many carpet tiles will be needed?   (2)

The carpet tiles can be bought in boxes of ten for £28 a box, or singly at £3.50 each.

(iii) What will be the cost of the carpet tiles to cover the floor?   (2)

(iv)   What do you think is the best way to buy the tiles?   (1)

3.44 The charges at a car park are shown on the sign below.

> **PARKING FEES**
> Up to 1 hour: £1
> 1 to 2 hours: £2
> 2 to 5 hours: £5
> FINE for exceeding the time limit £20 per hour
> Parking between 18:00 and 07:30 free

Mr Gordon parked at 09:55 and took 13 minutes, as always, to walk the distance between the car park and the hairdresser. His haircut always took 35 minutes.

(i)   What fee did he need to pay at the car park to be sure he didn't get a fine?   (2)

Mrs McKay didn't have any £1 coins so she paid £2 with a £2 coin. She parked at 10:37 and returned 48 minutes later.

(ii)   How much time was left before the ticket expired?   (2)

Lord Grabbitt parked his Rolls Royce at 16:05 and went to the cinema to watch a film lasting two and a half hours.

(iii)   How much did he need to pay?   (2)

3.45 Lizzie is planning to paint the four walls of her bedroom. The room is 5 metres square and 3 metres high. Lizzie calculates that the door and window have a total area of 4 square metres.

(i)   What area does Lizzie plan to paint?   (2)

She chooses pink paint, which is sold in 5-litre tins costing £18.99 and in 2-litre tins costing £9.99

The instructions say that 1 litre will be sufficient to give two coats of paint to an area of 7 square metres. Lizzie intends to give the walls two coats of paint.

(ii)   How many litres of paint are needed?   (2)

(iii)   What size or sizes of tin should Lizzie buy, and what will the cost be?   (2)

3.46 In his collection, Sebastian has a Roman denarius coin of the emperor Nerva, who was in power from 18 September 96 A.D. to 25 January 98 A.D.

> *The calendar that the Romans used was very confusing and several important changes were made during the last half century B.C.! During the time of Nerva, the months had the same names and numbers of days as they do now, and 97 A.D. was not a leap year!*

(i)   For how many days was Nerva in power?   (3)

Sebastian paid £60 for the coin and another collector has offered him £150 for it.

(ii)   If Sebastian decides to sell the coin for £150 how much profit will he make?   (1)

(iii)   What will Sebastian's profit be as a percentage of his purchase price?   (2)

Challenge 3K

The Romans didn't use our numerals 0, 1, …, 8, 9 when representing numbers.

Nerva came to power in the year XCVI A.D.

It is interesting to look again at some of the questions in this book with all the numbers rewritten in Roman numerals. For example:

1.09 (i)   Here is a sequence.

XIII   XVIII   XXIII   XXVIII   XXXIII   ….   ….

Copy the sequence and write down the next two terms.

1.33 Seven number cards are shown below.

Answer the questions on page 13

Answer some of the other questions in this book, rewriting all the numbers in Roman numerals.

Challenge 3L

At first, the Romans used IIII to represent four and VIIII to represent nine. Later, they introduced IV (one before five) and IX (one before ten). This means that in these numbers the numeral I really represents 'negative one'. This is a clever idea, but it makes operations with Roman numerals more difficult!

Study these examples using the earlier system of IIII and VIIII and so on, without negative numbers:

(i)   XXIII (23) + XVII (17) gives us XXXVIIIII, but IIIII is the same as V and then VV is the same as X, so the sum of the two numbers is XXXX (40).

(ii)   LXXII (72) – XXXXVI (46) is a little more tricky. We can change the L into XXXXX and change one X into two Vs to give XXXXXXVVII (still 72) and then subtract XXXXVI to give XXVI (26).

(iii)   XXIII (23) × VII (7) is perhaps easier! We know that V × I is V, and V × X is L, so we get XXIII + XXIII + LLVVV (V × XXIII). This gives LLXXXXXVVVIIIIII. This simplifies (by combining five Is to make a V, then four Vs to make two Xs, then five Xs to make an L, then two L's to make a C) to CLLXI (161).

Try some examples yourself.

4 ALGEBRA

4.1 EQUATIONS AND FORMULAE

Questions involving

- **word formulae**
- **expressions**
- **equations**

4.01 The diagram shows an equilateral triangle of side length s.

A word formula for the perimeter, p, of the shape could be written as

'perimeter = 3 times length of side'

or, more simply, as $p = 3s$

We can represent this by a flowchart.

$$\text{side length } (s) \longrightarrow \boxed{\times\, 3} \longrightarrow \text{perimeter } (p)$$

Calculate the perimeter of an equilateral triangle of side length

(i)   3 cm   (1)

(ii)   5 cm   (1)

(iii) $2\frac{1}{2}$ cm   (1)

We can add to the flowchart, as shown below.

$$\text{side length } (s) \quad \genfrac{}{}{0pt}{}{\boxed{\times\, 3}}{\boxed{\div\, 3}} \quad \text{perimeter } (p)$$

Calculate the side length of an equilateral triangle with perimeter

(iv)   12 cm   (1)

(v)   18 cm   (1)

(vi) $4\frac{1}{2}$ cm   (1)

4.02 Fatima has given the following instructions as a word formula:

'Think of a number, add 3, multiply by 4, subtract 12, add the number you first thought of and finally divide by 5'.

Following Fatima's instructions, write down each step and the result when the starting number is

(i)   2   (1)

(ii)   5   (1)

(iii)   10   (1)

(iv)   any number you choose!   (1)

(v)   Represent Fatima's word formula as a flowchart.   (2)

Challenge 4A

You might like to find out how Fatima's puzzle works! You could make up a similar puzzle to try out on your friends.

4.03 The diagram below shows a regular hexagon of side length s.

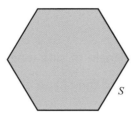

s

(i)   Write a word formula to calculate the perimeter, p, of the shape.   (1)

Calculate the perimeter of a regular hexagon of side length

(ii)   3 cm   (1)

(iii)   5 cm   (1)

(iv) $2\frac{1}{2}$ cm.   (1)

Calculate the side length of a regular hexagon with perimeter

(v)   12 cm   (1)

(vi)   9 cm.   (1)

4.04 (a)   On an ordinary die, the numbers on opposite faces always have a sum of 7, so if the number on the top face is 6, the number on the bottom face is 1

    (i)   Write down the number on the bottom face when the number on the top face is 3   (1)

    (ii)   Using t for the number on the top face and b for the number on the bottom face, copy and complete this formula to find the bottom number.

        $b = \ldots$ (2)

(b)   The cost of an ice-cream is 75 pence. The formula $c = 75n$ helps to calculate the total cost, c, in pence, of any number, n, of ice-creams.

    (i)   Use the formula to calculate the cost of ten ice-creams.   (1)

    (ii)   What is the cost, in pounds, of ten ice-creams?   (1)

    The total cost, C, in pounds, of n ice-creams can be found by using the formula

    $C = \frac{75n}{100}$

    (iii)   Copy and complete the flowchart below to represent the word formula.   (1)

$$n \rightarrow \boxed{\times} \rightarrow \boxed{} \rightarrow C$$

4.05 The word formula *'Denise thought of a number, d, multiplied it by 3 and then added 4'* can be represented by the flowchart below.

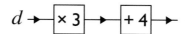

Since we do not know what number Denise thought of, we have represented her number by the letter *d*.

Write down the result if the number Denise thought of was

(i)	3	(1)
(ii)	6	(1)
(iii)	11	(1)

Write down the number Denise thought of, if the result was

(iv)	19	(1)
(v)	28	(1)
(vi)	1	(1)

4.06 Erin thought of a number, *e*, added 3 and then multiplied by 2

(i)	Draw a flowchart to represent this.	(1)

Write down the result if the number Erin thought of was

(ii)	3	(1)
(iii)	6	(1)

Write down the number Erin thought of, if the result was

(iv)	16	(1)
(v)	22	(1)
(vi)	4	(1)

4.07 Faisal thought of a number, subtracted 3 and then multiplied by 5

(i)	Draw a flowchart to represent this.	(1)

Write down the result if the number Faisal thought of was

(ii)	3	(1)
(iii)	2	(1)

Write down the number Faisal thought of, if the result was

(iv)	20	(1)
(v)	25	(1)
(vi)	5	(1)

4.08 The line below measures 7.5 cm. This is approximately the same as 3 inches.

If your ruler is marked in inches as well as centimetres, you will notice that 30 cm (4 times 7.5 cm) is approximately the same as 12 inches (4 times 3 inches).

If a ruler is marked only in centimetres and we need to know a measurement in inches, we could use the word formula *'multiply by 12 and then divide by 30'*.

(i)   Draw a flowchart to represent this word formula.   (1)

Use the word formula to find the equivalent measurement in inches of

(ii)   15 cm   (1)

(iii)   25 cm.   (1)

(iv)   Write a word formula which will give instructions for converting from inches to centimetres.   (1)

Use the word formula to find the equivalent measurement in centimetres of

(v)   8 inches   (1)

(vi)   9 inches.   (1)

4.09 Graham is thinking of a number which he calls g.

Harriet is thinking of a number which is 4 more than Graham's number.

(i)   Write an expression, in terms of g, for Harriet's number.   (1)

Isla is thinking of a number which is 3 times Graham's number.

(ii)   Write an expression, in terms of g, for Isla's number.   (1)

James is thinking of a number which is 2 less than Graham's number.

(iii)   Write an expression, in terms of g, for James's number.   (1)

Write a expression, in terms of g and simplified if possible, for the sum of

(iv)   Graham's number and Harriet's number   (1)

(v)   Graham's number and Isla's number   (1)

(vi)   all four numbers.   (1)

4.10 Robbie, Stuart and Trisha are thinking of three numbers, r, s and t.

They write expressions using their numbers and then tell everyone what their numbers are: $r = 4$, $s = 9$ and $t = 2$

By substitution, find the value of each of the following expressions.

(i) $r + s$ (1)

(ii) $2r + t$ (1)

(iii) $r + s - t$ (1)

(iv) $3r - s + 4t$ (1)

(v) rs (1)

(vi) $t(s - r)$ (1)

4.11 If $u = 3$, $v = 5$ and $w = {}^-2$, find the value of each of the following expressions.

    (i) $u + v$ (1)

    (ii) $v + w$ (1)

    (iii) $v - u$ (1)

    (iv) $v - w$ (1)

    (v) $v + uw$ (1)

    (vi) $v - uw$ (1)

4.12 (a)   Katrin thought of a number, k, multiplied it by 5 and then added 2

        (i)   Write an expression, in terms of k, for the result.   (1)

        (ii)   If Katrin thought of 4, what was the result?   (1)

    (b)   Jamie thought of a number, j, added 2 and then multiplied by 5

        (i)   Write an expression, in terms of j, for the result.   (1)

        (ii)   If Jamie's result was 30, what number did he think of?   (1)

    (c)   Moira thought of a number, m, multiplied it by 3 and then subtracted 4

        (i)   Write an expression, in terms of m, for the result.   (1)

        (ii)   If Moira's result was the number she first thought of, what number did she think of?   (1)

4.13 Find the number represented by the symbol ◆ in the each of the following number sentences.

    (i) $21 + ◆ = 23$ (1)

    (ii) $◆ - 13 = 9$ (1)

    (iii) $7 × ◆ = 84$ (1)

    (iv) $3 × ◆ × 8 = 48$ (1)

    (v) $37 + ◆ = 6 × 9$ (1)

    (vi) $18 - ◆ = 4 + ◆$ (in this part, the same mystery number appears twice)   (1)

4.14 Find the numbers represented by the letters in these equations.

    (i) $a + 7 = 23$ (1)

    (ii) $b - 9 = 14$ (1)

    (iii) $6c = 30$ (1)

    (iv) $4d - 6 = 14$ (1)

    (v) $2(e + 2) = 12$ (1)

    (vi) $3f + 5 = f + 7$ (1)

4.15 Solve the following equations.

    (i) $x + 8 = 13$ (1)

    (ii) $4x = 24$ (1)

    (iii) $3x - 4 = 11$ (1)

    (iv) $2x + 5 = 7$ (1)

    (v) $x + 6 = 4$ (1)

    (vi) $\dfrac{x}{4} = 8$ (1)

4.2 SEQUENCES AND FUNCTIONS

Questions involving

● sequences
● function machines

4.16 (a)   Gerry has a machine which adds 7 to every input number.

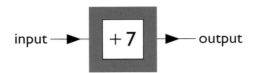

Write down the output when Gerry puts in

(i)   4   (1)

(ii)   13   (1)

(b)   Hugo has the machine illustrated below.

Write down the output when Hugo puts in

(i)   5   (1)

(ii)   1   (1)

(c)   Imogen has the machine below.

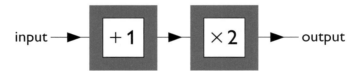

Write down the output when Imogen puts in

(i)   5   (1)

(ii)   1   (1)

Challenge 4B

Choose two labels of your own for a machine, for example × 5 (A) and + 4 (B).

On a copy of the machine, write the labels A, then B, and find the outputs for two input numbers (such as 5 and 1).

On a second copy of the machine, write the same labels, in the order B then A, and find the outputs for the same input numbers.

The order of the operations is important!

4.17 Function machines can be used to generate sequences.

(a)   Consider the simple 'add 3' machine shown below. If the output is fed back into the machine over and over again, the following sequence is generated.

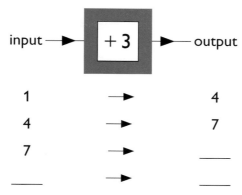

input		output
1	→	4
4	→	7
7	→	___
___	→	___

(i)   Copy and complete the table of input and output values above.   (1)

(ii)   Copy the sequence generated and write down the next three terms.   (1)

(b)   Copy and complete the table for the 'multiply by 3' machine shown below.   (2)

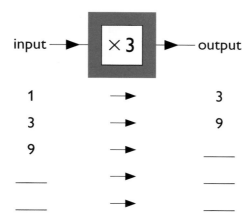

input		output
1	→	3
3	→	9
9	→	___
___	→	___
___	→	___

(c)   Starting with the input 1, write down the first four terms generated, in the same way, by a 'subtract 2' machine.   (2)

Challenge 4C

(i)   On a blank copy of the machine used in 4.17, write your own label, for example – 5, and then choose a suitable starting input number, such as 23

Using the idea in question 4.17, generate the sequence of numbers.

(ii)   Look at question 1.09 on page 4 and decide which machine would generate each of the sequences.

4.18 (a)   The function machine below consists of two functions.

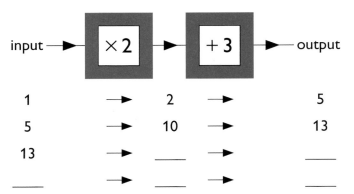

(i)   Copy and complete the table of input and output values above.   (2)

(ii)   Copy the sequence below and write down the next four terms.   (2)

$$1 \longrightarrow 5 \longrightarrow 13 \longrightarrow \dots$$

(b)   The function machine below consists of the same two functions in a different order.

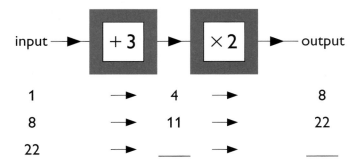

Copy the sequence generated and write down the next four terms.   (2)

$$1 \longrightarrow 8 \longrightarrow 22 \longrightarrow \dots$$

4.19 (a)   The label has fallen off the machine below.

The machine is known to generate the following sequence.

$$1 \longrightarrow 6 \longrightarrow 11 \longrightarrow 16 \longrightarrow \dots$$

(i)   What label should be on the machine?   (1)

(ii)   Write the next two terms of the sequence.   (1)

(b)   One label has fallen off the two-stage function machine below.

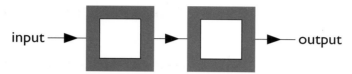

The machine is known to generate the following sequence.

1 ⟶ 6 ⟶ 16 ⟶ 36 ⟶ ...

(i)   What should the second label be?   (1)

(ii)   Write the next two terms of the sequence.   (1)

(c)   Both labels have fallen off the two-stage machine below!

input ⟶ ☐ ⟶ ☐ ⟶ output

The machine is known to generate the following sequence.

1 ⟶ 8 ⟶ 22 ⟶ 50 ⟶ ...

What labels would generate this sequence?   (2)

Challenge 4D

Suggest alternative labels that would generate the same sequence in question (c).

Challenge 4E

The 8 labels below have fallen off four 2-function machines (like those in question 4.19 above)!

| ×3 | ×2 | +3 | +2 | +1 | −3 | −2 | −1 |

Machine A generates the sequence

1 ⟶ 4 ⟶ 13 ⟶ 40 ⟶ ...

Machine B generates the sequence

1 ⟶ 4 ⟶ 12 ⟶ 28 ⟶ ...

Which 2 labels, in which order, should be on (i) Machine A and (ii) Machine B?

You might like to make up machines which use the other 4 labels.

4.3 GRAPHS

Questions involving

● the co-ordinate grid, including plotting points
● shapes drawn on a grid
● linear functions represented on a grid

4.20 Function machines can be used to produce ordered pairs of numbers. Here we do not feed the output back into the machine but simply look at pairs of input and output numbers.

(i)   Copy and complete the table of input and output numbers for the 'add 2' machine below. (2)

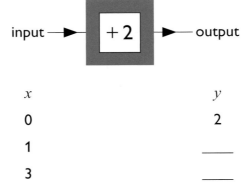

x	y
0	2
1	___
3	___
___	8

(ii) On a copy of the co-ordinate grid below, plot the ordered pairs of input (x) and output (y) numbers. (2)

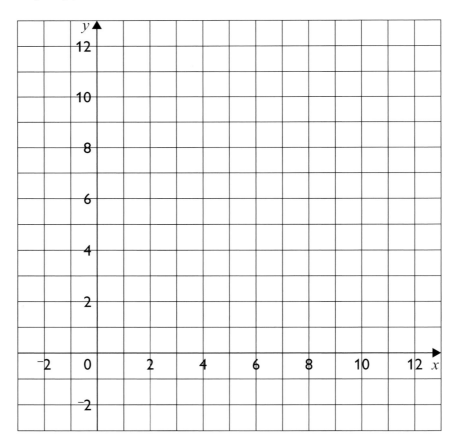

(iii) Draw a straight line through your points. (1)

(iv) Write down, in the form $y = \ldots$, the equation of the line you have drawn. (1)

4.21 A graph is drawn on the grid below.

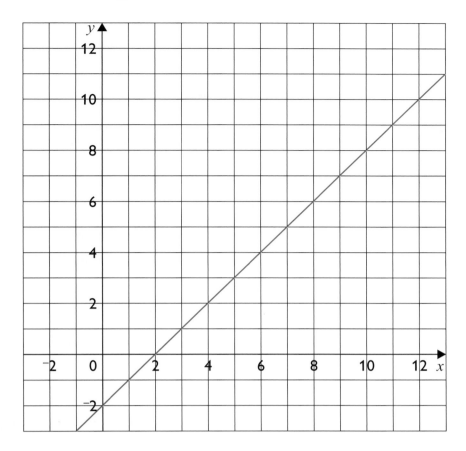

(i)   Copy the diagram and mark, with crosses, the points on the graph which
        have x co-ordinates of 2, 6, 10 and 12   (1)

(ii)   Write the co-ordinates of the four points as ordered pairs, for example (2, 0).   (1)

(iii) What is the equation of the line in the form $y = \dots$?   (1)

(iv)   On your copy of the grid, plot suitable points and draw a graph to represent the
       function $y = x + 4$ (2)

(v)   What do you notice about the graphs of the functions above?   (1)

4.22 The two function machines A and B below are used to make ordered pairs of numbers.

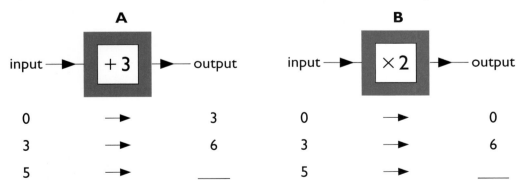

(i)   Copy and complete the tables of input and output numbers above.   (1)

(ii)   On a co-ordinate grid, plot the ordered pairs of input (x) and output (y) numbers
        for the two machines.   (2)

(iii) Draw and label the graphs of the two functions.   (2)

(iv)   What are the co-ordinates of the point of intersection of the two lines?   (1)

4.23 The two-stage function machine below is used to make ordered pairs of numbers.

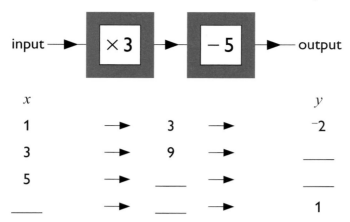

x				y
1	→	3	→	⁻2
3	→	9	→	____
5	→	____	→	____
____	→	____	→	1

   (i)   Copy and complete the table of input and output numbers above.   (2)

   (ii)   On a co-ordinate grid, plot the ordered pairs of input (x) and output (y) numbers.   (2)

   (iii) Draw the graph of this two-stage function.   (1)

   (iv) What is the equation of the line?   (1)

4.24 You may remember (see question 4.04) that on an ordinary die, the numbers on opposite faces always have a sum of 7

The function machine below can provide a series of ordered pairs of numbers.

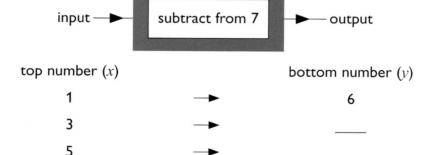

top number (x)		bottom number (y)
1	→	6
3	→	____
5	→	____

   (i)   Copy and complete the table of values above.   (1)

   (ii)   Copy and complete this list of six ordered pairs.

       $(1, 6), (2, 5), (3,$ ____ $), \ldots$ (1)

   (iii) On a co-ordinate grid mark, with crosses, the points representing these ordered pairs.   (2)

   (iv) What is the equation, in the form $y = \ldots$, of the line on which all of these points lie?   (2)

4.25 On the grid below, lines A and B have been drawn.

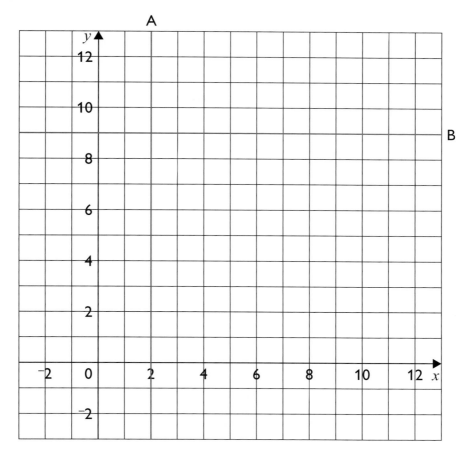

Write down the equation of

(i)   line A   (1)

(ii) line B.   (1)

On a copy of the grid above, draw and label

(iii) line C with equation $y = 5$ (1)

(iv)   line D with equation $x = 6$ (1)

(v)   Shade the area bounded by the four lines and name the shaded shape.   (1)

(vi)   Write down the co-ordinates of the mid-point of the shaded shape.   (1)

4.26 (i)   On a co-ordinate grid, plot the points with co-ordinates $(3, 4)$, $(^-1, 9)$, $(3, 11)$, $(7, 9)$. (2)

(ii)   Join the points, in order, to form a shape and shade the shape.   (1)

(iii) Name the shaded shape.   (1)

(iv)   What is the area, in square units, of the shaded shape?   (2)

4.27 Two shapes are shown on the co-ordinate grid below.

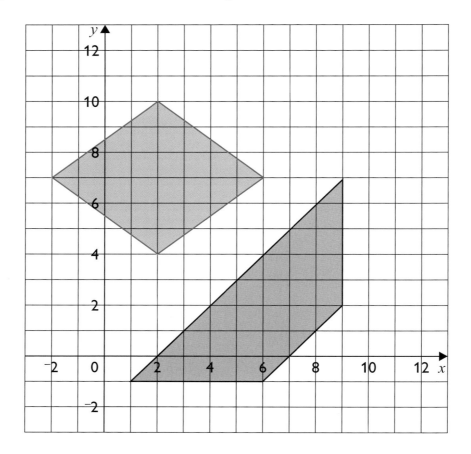

Write down the co-ordinates of the vertices (corners) of

(i)   the orange shape   (1)

(ii)   the grey shape.   (1)

Name

(iii)   the orange shape   (1)

(iv)   the grey shape.   (1)

(v)   What are the equations of the lines of symmetry of the orange shape?   (1)

(vi)   What is the equation of the line of symmetry of the grey shape?   (1)

4.28 On a co-ordinate grid, draw and label the lines with the following equations.

(i) $y = x + 4$ (2)

(ii) $y = 2x$ (2)

(iii) $y = 2x - 4$ (2)

Challenge 4F

On a co-ordinate grid, draw the line with equation $y = 8 - x$.

---

5 SHAPE, SPACE AND MEASURES

5.1 MEASURES

Questions involving

- **length and distance, including perimeters**
- **mass**
- **temperature**
- **area**
- **capacity and volume**
- **time**
- **speed**
- **reading scales**

5.01 (a)   Consider the units:

mm   cm   m   km

Using appropriate units, write down an estimate of

(i)   the length of a mobile phone   (1)

(ii)   the distance you could walk, at normal walking speed, in an hour   (1)

(iii)   the thickness of a £1 coin.   (1)

(b)   Consider the units:

mm²   cm²   m²   ha (hectare)   km²

Using appropriate units, write down an estimate of the area of

(i)   a page of this book   (1)

(ii)   a hole-punch hole in a sheet of paper   (1)

(iii)   a tennis court.   (1)

5.02 (a)   (i)   Measure the perimeter, in millimetres, of this regular
                          hexagon.   (1)

(ii)   What would be the quickest way of finding this perimeter?   (1)

(b)   For the rectangle below, calculate

(i)   the perimeter   7 cm   (1)

(ii)   the area.   (1)

2.5 cm

(c)   For the shape below, calculate

(i)   the perimeter   (1)

(ii)   the area.   9 cm   (1)

1 cm

2 cm

Not to scale

6 cm

5.03 (a) Consider the units:

mm³   cm³   m³   ml   litre

Using appropriate units, write down an estimate of

(i)   the capacity of a tea cup (1)

(ii) the volume of a 1p coin (1)

(iii) the capacity of a bath. (1)

(b) Consider the units:

mg   g   kg   tonne

Using appropriate units, write down an estimate of the mass of

(i)   a Labrador dog (1)

(ii) a £2 coin (1)

(iii) a drawing pin. (1)

5.04 (a) Two identical measuring cylinders are shown here.

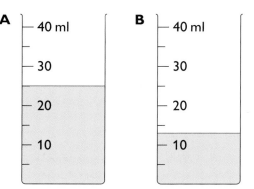

(i)   What is the volume of liquid in cylinder A? (1)

(ii) Estimate the volume of liquid in cylinder B. (1)

(iii) If liquid was poured from cylinder A into B until the levels were the same, what volume of liquid would be in each cylinder? (1)

(b) (i) What is the mass, in kilograms, of Emma's dog Poppy, recorded on the weighing scales opposite? (1)

(ii) If Poppy's mass increases by 3.8 kg, what will be the reading on the scales then? (1)

(c) Two readings, C and D, are shown on the Celsius temperature scale below.

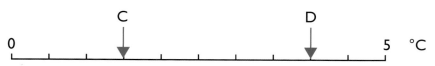

How many degrees warmer is reading D than reading C? (1)

5.05 (a)   Joanne has a 2 litre bottle of lemonade and fills as many 150 ml glasses as possible.

(i)   How many glasses can she fill?   (1)

(ii)   What volume of lemonade will be left in the bottle?   (1)

(b)   Picture framing can be bought in 2.4 m lengths. Arthur needs two 0.9 m lengths and two 0.4 m lengths.

(i)   How many 2.4 m lengths of framing will Arthur need to buy?   (1)

(ii)   What total length of framing will be left?   (1)

(iii)   What is the longest possible piece he could have left?   (2)

5.06 (a)   Amy's height is 1.05 m Write her height

(i)   in centimetres   (1)

(ii)   in millimetres   (1)

(iii)   in feet and inches.   (1)

(b)   Amy's mass is 30 kg. Write her mass

(i)   in grams   (1)

(ii)   in pounds   (1)

(iii)   in stones and pounds.   (1)

Challenge 5A

In question 5.06(b), Amy's mass is 30 kg. Imagine Amy being lowered to the bottom of the deepest hole on Earth. Her mass will remain the same, but her weight will increase slightly because the pull of gravity is greater nearer to the centre of the Earth. If instead she is taken up in a hot air balloon, her weight will decrease slightly. If she went far enough above the surface of the Earth, she would become 'weightless'!

At the surface of the Earth, Amy's weight is about 300 N (300 newtons).

Find the masses (in mg, g or kg) of some objects and write down the weights in newtons.

When people talk about 'losing weight', they really mean 'losing mass'!

Challenge 5B

Collect ten objects, for example: spoon, stone, book, plate, bucket, football, and so on. First, arrange the objects in order of increasing mass and then estimate the masses of the objects. If possible, see how accurate your estimates are.

Collect ten containers. Arrange them in order of increasing capacity. Some of your containers (such as drinks bottles) will probably have known capacities which will help you to estimate the capacities of the other containers.

5.07 The isometric drawing below shows a cuboid made from centimetre cubes.

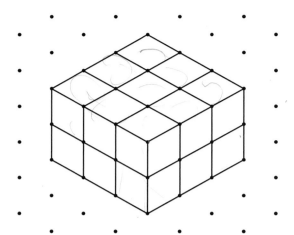

For this cuboid write down

(i) the volume (1)

(ii) the area of the top face (1)

(iii) the total surface area. (1)

How many cuboids, identical to the one above, could be fitted into a box measuring

(iv) 3 cm by 3 cm by 12 cm (1)

(v) 6 cm by 6 cm by 6 cm? (1)

(vi) How many little cuboids each measuring 1 cm by 1 cm by 2 cm could be made from the cuboid illustrated above? (1)

5.08 (i) Write down the temperature shown on Theo's thermometer below. (1)

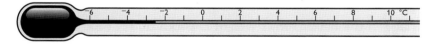

What would the thermometer record if the temperature

(ii) fell 3 degrees (1)

(iii) rose 4.5 degrees? (1)

Theo uses the word formula 'divide by 5, then multiply by 9 and finally add 32' to convert from degrees Celsius to degrees Fahrenheit.

What is the Fahrenheit equivalent of

(iv) 15 °C (1)

(v) 25 °C (1)

(vi) ⁻2.5 °C? (1)

5.09 (a) Write these as 24-hour times:

      (i)   8.00 a.m. (1)

      (ii)   8.00 p.m. (1)

(b) Write these as a.m./p.m. times:

      (i)   14:45 (1)

      (ii)   21.05 (1)

(c) Corrie's watch is 3 minutes fast and Donald's watch is 4 minutes slow.

When Corrie's watch reads 15:01, what will Donald's watch read? (1)

(d) Raymond's old watch gains 30 seconds in 24 hours. If he sets his watch at exactly the right time on Monday at 08:00:00, what time will the watch read at 08:00:00 the following Monday? (1)

5.10 (a) Jade and Mishal ran in a 400 m race. Jade beat Mishal's time, which was 59.7 seconds, by 2.9 seconds. What was Jade's time? (1)

(b) Sam cycled 20 kilometres in 1 hour 20 minutes, at a steady speed.

How far did he cycle

      (i)   in 10 minutes (1)

      (ii)   in 1 hour? (1)

(c) A coach left Loveham at 09:55 and reached Hateham at 13:25

      (i)   How long did the journey take? (1)

The coach travelled at a steady speed of 70 km/hour.

      (ii) How many kilometres is it from Loveham to Hateham? (2)

5.11 Sarah's snail, Slimy Supersnail, is shown in the picture below.

Slimy slides 2 cm in 12 minutes.

At this speed, how far could Slimy slide

(i)   in 1 hour (1)

(ii)   in 30 minutes? (1)

How long would it take Slimy to slide

(iii) 1 metre (1)

(iv) 1 kilometre? (1)

(v) Assuming that Slimy Supersnail does not run out of stamina or slime, how many years, approximately, would it take him to slide, non-stop, the 1400 km from Land's End to John O'Groats? (2)

5.12 (a) Amelia has made a cuboid measuring 5 cm by 3 cm by 3 cm, by gluing centimetre cubes together.

For Amelia's cuboid, write down

    (i)   the volume   (1)

    (ii)   the area of the largest face.   (1)

  (b) The diagram below shows an isometric drawing of a solid made by gluing centimetre cubes together.

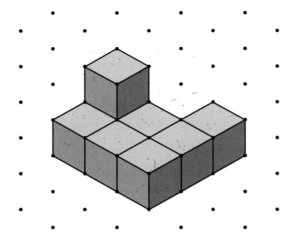

    (i)   How many centimetre cubes have been used to make the solid?   (1)

    (ii)   If the solid is painted all over (including the base), what area will be painted?   (2)

    (iii)   How many centimetre cubes would you need to add to this solid to make a cube with 3 cm edges?   (1)

Challenge 5C

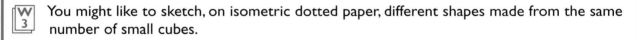

W 3   You might like to sketch, on isometric dotted paper, different shapes made from the same number of small cubes.

You might also like to try the following:

(i)   Make an imaginative solid from interlocking centimetre cubes and then, on isometric dotted paper, make a sketch of your solid.

(ii)   Sketch a solid on isometric dotted paper and then challenge a friend to make the solid from interlocking centimetre cubes.

5.2 SHAPE

Questions involving

● **plane shapes, including symmetry and congruence**
● **solid shapes, including isometric drawings and nets**

5.13 (a) Name the plane shapes A, B and C. (3)

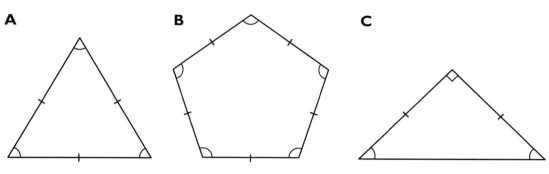

(b) Name the solid shapes D, E and F. (3)

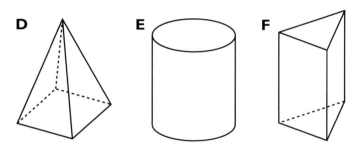

5.14 Ten plane shapes are drawn on the square dotted grid below.

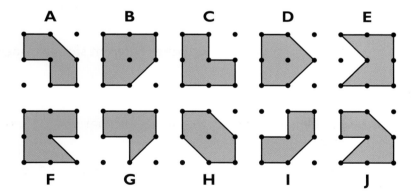

(i) Which shape has the same area as shape B? (1)

(ii) Which shape has exactly the same perimeter as shape H? (1)

(iii) Which two shapes are congruent? (1)

(iv) Which shape has two lines of symmetry? (1)

(v) List all the shapes which have one, and only one, line of symmetry. (2)

Challenge 5D

Each of the shapes A to J can be made from a 2 unit square by removing triangles and/or squares. See how many different (non-congruent) shapes can be made in the same way.

5.15 The shape below was made from a 10 cm square piece of card by cutting right-angled isosceles triangles from a pair of opposite corners.

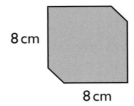

8 cm

8 cm

For this shape, write down

(i)   the name   (1)

(ii)   the number of lines of symmetry   (1)

(iii)   the order of rotational symmetry   (1)

(iv)   the area.   (1)

(v)   If the shape is cut in two along its longest diagonal, what shape is each half?   (1)

(vi)   Sketch the shape above and show how it could be cut to form a pentagon and an isosceles triangle.   (1)

5.16 The drawing below shows a cuboid made from thin card printed with a centimetre square grid.

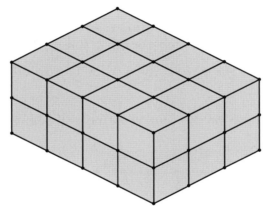

W 13 (i)   On centimetre squared or square dotted paper, draw a net of the cuboid.   (2)

W 16 For this cuboid, write down the total

(ii)   surface area   (1)

(iii)   length of all the edges.   (1)

W 3 (iv)   On isometric dotted paper, draw a view of the cuboid standing on one of its smallest faces.   (1)

(v)   How many planes of symmetry does the cuboid have?   (1)

5.17 On square dotted paper, name and draw an example of each of the quadrilaterals A, B and C
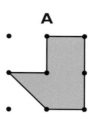 described below.

> (i)   A has two, and only two, lines of symmetry and equal sides.   (2)

> (ii)   B has equal diagonals and just one line of symmetry.   (2)

> (iii)   C has two pairs of equal sides and diagonals which cross at right angles.   (2)

5.18 The diagram below shows shape A drawn on a centimetre square dotted grid.

A

> (i)   On centimetre square dotted paper copy shape A and draw shape B, which is
>   a mirror image of shape A.   (1)

> (ii)   Now draw shape C, which is a half-turn rotation of shape A about one of its
>   vertices (corners).   (1)

> (iii)   What word describes the relationship between shapes A, B and C?   (1)

> (iv)   Draw shape D, which is similar to shapes A, B and C and where each side
>   of D is twice as long as the corresponding side of shape A.   (2)

> (v)   How many times larger is the area of shape D than the area of shapes A,
>   B and C?   (1)

5.19 Study the five shapes drawn on the square dotted grid below.

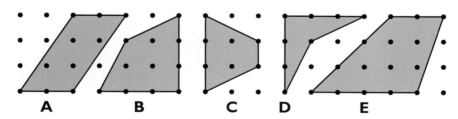

> (i)   Name each of the shapes B, C, D and E.   (2)

> (ii)   What word could be used to describe all of these shapes?   (1)

> (iii)   In what way is shape A different from all the others?   (1)

> (iv)   Which two shapes could be joined to form a square?   (1)

> (v)   Which two shapes have exactly the same perimeter?   (1)

Challenge 5E

The parallelogram (shape A) in question 5.19 has area 6 cm² (base 2 cm × 'height' 3 cm).

> (i)   On centimetre squared dotted paper, draw three different parallelograms with
>   area 6 cm².

> (ii)   Draw four different triangles with area 6 cm².

5.20 The diagram below shows the net of a solid shape drawn on an isometric dotted grid.

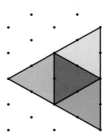

(i)   Name the solid shape which can be made from the net above.   (1)

For the completed shape, write down the number of

(ii)   faces   (1)

(iii) vertices   (1)

(iv) edges.   (1)

(v)   How many different coloured faces meet at each vertex?   (1)

Each edge of the completed shape is 2 units long. Sally makes the shape from the net above and then makes a similar shape where the length of each edge is 4 units.

(vi) How many times larger than the area of the net of the first shape is the area of the net of the larger shape?   (1)

5.21 Study the shape below.

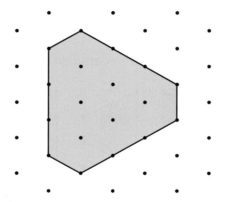

 (i) Copy the shape on centimetre isometric dotted paper, and on your copy draw all the lines of symmetry of the shape.   (1)

(ii) What is the order of rotational symmetry of the shape?   (1)

(iii) What is the perimeter of the shape?   (1)

(iv) On centimetre isometric dotted paper, draw a shape with the same symmetry properties and perimeter 18 cm.   (2)

The shape above has the same area as 22 equilateral triangles of side 1 cm.

(v) How many equilateral triangles of side 1 cm have the same area as the shape you have drawn in part (iv)?   (1)

Challenge 5F

This could be a good starting point for an investigation. For example, you might like to see how many different hexagons with the same area you could draw.

5.22 Two views of the same solid shape made from centimetre cubes are shown on the isometric grid below.

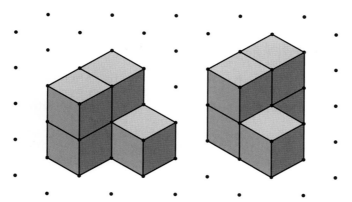

(i) Describe the symmetry of the shape. (1)

(ii) What is the total surface area of the shape? (1)

 (iii) On isometric dotted paper draw two more views of the same solid. (4)

5.3 SPACE

Questions involving

- angles and angle facts
- the eight-point compass and bearings
- scale drawings
- transformations: reflection, rotation and translation
- triangle construction

5.23 (a) What name is given to an angle which is

(i) less than a right angle (1)

(ii) more than a half-turn (1)

(iii) between 90° and 180°? (1)

(b) Without measuring, list the angles a, b and c in order of increasing size. (2)

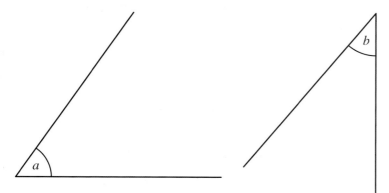 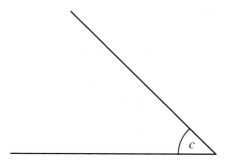

(c) If one angle of a triangle is a right angle, what name would be given to each of the other two angles? (1)

5.24 *For each part of this question, you may find it helpful to draw a sketch.*

    (a)   Two angles of a triangle are 40° and 70°.

        (i)   What is the third angle?   (1)

        (ii)   What type of triangle is this?   (1)

    (b)   One angle of a parallelogram is 40°. What are the other three angles?   (1)

    (c)   One angle of an isosceles trapezium is 80°. What are the other three angles?   (1)

    (d)   Two adjacent angles of a kite are 80°. What are the other two angles?   (2)

5.25 (a)   Consider the diagrams below.

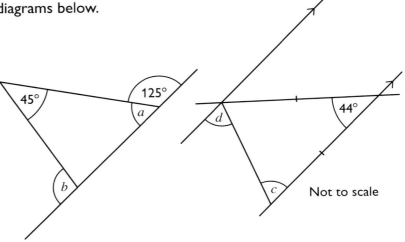

    Calculate the size of

    (i)   angle a (1)

    (ii)   angle b (1)

    (iii)   angle c (1)

    (iv)   angle d.   (1)

    (b)   If two of the three angles around a point are 148° and 109°, what is the third angle? (1)

    (c)   If the sizes of three angles around a point are in the ratio 1 : 2 : 5, what is the smallest angle?   (1)

5.26 (a)   Measure and write down the sizes of the angles drawn below.   (3)

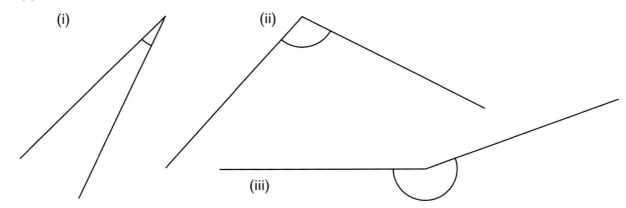

    (b)   Draw and label the following angles.

        (i)   40°   (1)

        (ii)   125°   (1)

        (iii)   87°   (1)

5.27 (i)   In the centre of a page, draw a line AB of length 10 cm.   (1)

(ii)   With centre A, draw an arc of radius 6 cm.   (1)

(iii)   With centre B, draw an arc of radius 8 cm.   (1)

(iv)   Mark the point where the arcs intersect, C, and complete the drawing of triangle ABC.   (1)

Measure and write down the size of

(v)   angle ACB (1)

(vi)   angle ABC.   (1)

Challenge 5G

Draw a kite which has sides of length 6 cm and 9 cm and the longest diagonal 10 cm.

5.28 (i)   In the centre of a page, draw a line DE of length 8.5 cm.   (1)

(ii)   At D, measure angle EDF of 40° and draw a line DF of length 8.5 cm.   (1)

(iii)   Draw EF and write down the length EF.   (1)

Measure and write down the size of

(iv)   angle DEF (1)

(v)   angle DFE.   (1)

(vi)   Draw a line of symmetry of triangle DEF.   (1)

Challenge 5H

Draw a triangle where the longest side measures 10 cm, the shortest side measures 5.5 cm and the smallest angle measures 30°.

Is there more than one possible triangle?

5.29 (i)   In the centre of a page, draw a line GH of length 9.8 cm.   (1)

(ii)   At G, measure angle HGI of 50° and draw the second arm of the angle as long as possible on the page.   (1)

(iii)   At H, measure angle GHI of 40° and draw the second arm of the angle as long as possible on the page.   (1)

(iv)   Mark the point of intersection of the lines drawn in (ii) and (iii), I, and measure angle GIH.   (1)

Measure and write down the length of

(v) GI (1)

(vi) HI.   (1)

5.30 (i)   Construct an equilateral triangle ABC of side 8 cm.   (2)

(ii)   Draw all the lines of symmetry of triangle ABC and mark the point of intersection, P.   (1)

(iii)   Measure and write down the distance PA.   (1)

(iv)   With centre P, draw a circle of radius PA.   (1)

(v)   With centres A, B and C, draw three circles of radius PA.   (1)

5.31 (a)   Copy the diagram below and on your copy reflect the shape in the line.   (2)

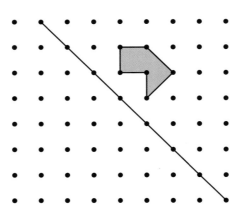

(b)   Copy the diagram below and on your copy rotate the shape 90° anticlockwise about the large dot.   (2)

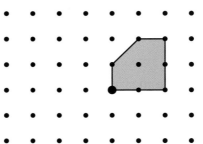

(c)   Copy the diagram below and on your copy translate the shape 3 units right and 2 units up.   (2)

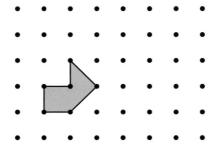

5.32 (i) Write down the co-ordinates of the vertices of triangle A shown in the diagram below. (1)

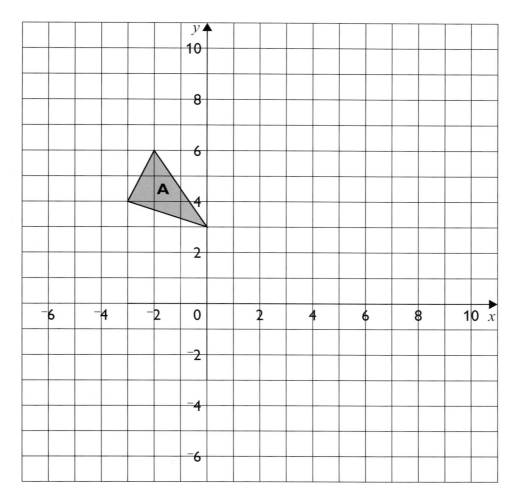

 (ii) Copy the diagram above and then reflect triangle A in the *x*-axis and label the image triangle B. (1)

(iii) Rotate triangle A through 180° about the point (⁻2, 6) and label the image triangle C. (1)

(iv) Translate triangle A 9 units to the right and 5 units down. Label the image triangle D. (1)

(v) Draw the line *x* = 3 and reflect triangle A in the line. Label the image triangle E. (1)

(vi) Rotate triangle A through 90° clockwise about the point (0, 1) and label the image triangle F. (1)

Challenge 51

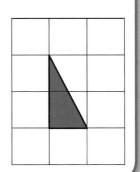

On a co-ordinate grid, cut out two congruent right-angled triangles like the one shown on the right. Label both sides of one triangle A and both sides of the other triangle B and colour both sides of each triangle.

Position your two cut-out triangles so that A would map onto B by reflection, rotation or translation and challenge a friend to say what the transformation is.

5.33 The diagram on the right shows the plan of a square lawn marked with a square grid of pegs placed 1 metre apart and lines representing the eight main compass directions.

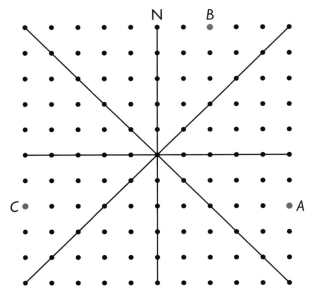

Copy the diagram above on square dotted paper and label the compass directions with

   (i)   letters (for example SW)   (1)

   (ii)   bearings (for example 090°).   (2)

   (iii)   Asha is standing at the peg marked A. She walks 6 metres west and then 4 metres north. On your copy, draw lines to show Asha's journey.   (1)

   Brian is standing at the peg marked *B* and Colin is standing at the peg marked *C*. Write down

   (iv)   the bearing of Colin from Brian   (1)

   (v)   the distance between them, to the nearest metre.   (1)

5.34 (a)   The diagram on the right shows three people, Julie, Kyle and Liam, and the directions in which they are facing.

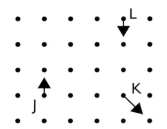

   Through what angle should

   (i)   Julie turn clockwise until she is facing Liam   (1)

   (ii)   Kyle turn clockwise until he is facing Julie?   (1)

For the rest of this question you may find it helpful to draw diagrams on square dotted paper.

   (b)   Mike is facing west. Norman is facing east and is standing due south of Mike.

   Through what angle should

   (i)   Mike turn clockwise until he is facing Norman   (1)

   (ii)   Norman turn anticlockwise until he is facing Mike?   (1)

   (c)   Olive is facing south-east and is standing due west of Polly, who is facing north-east.

   Through what angle should

   (i)   Olive turn clockwise until she is facing Polly   (1)

   (ii)   Polly turn anticlockwise until she is facing Olive?   (1)

5.35 The diagram below shows how a shape can be used to make a tessellation to fill a rectangle 6 cm by 5 cm.

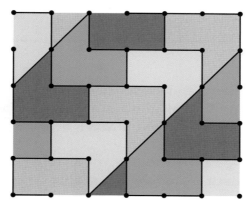

 On squared or square dotted paper, draw tessellations, within 6 cm by 5 cm rectangles, of

(i)   shape A   (3)

(ii)   shape B.   (3)

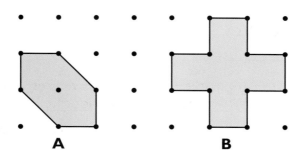

| A | B |

Challenge 5J

You might like to draw some interesting tessellations of other shapes. This could include tessellations which use two different shapes. Could you draw a tessellation which uses shape B and a square?

5.36 The diagram shows a fenced rectangular garden measuring 12 m by 6 m.

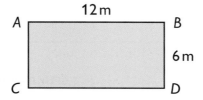

(i)   Using a scale of 1 : 100, make a scale drawing of the garden.   (2)

A goat, Gertrude, is tied to a post at A by a 5 m length of rope.

(ii)   Shade the area of the garden that Gertrude can reach.   (2)

A second goat, Grumpy, is tied to a post at the mid-point of CD by a 5 m length of rope.

(iii)   Shade, in a different colour, the area of the garden that cannot be reached by either goat.   (2)

6 HANDLING DATA

6.1 DATA HANDLING

Questions involving

- raw data, including tally charts and frequency tables
- representing data, including Carroll and Venn diagrams, pictograms, block graphs, bar charts, frequency diagrams and pie charts
- grouping data into class intervals
- interpreting data, including range, median, mode and mean
- representing continuous data, including line graphs

6.01 Study the information in the table below.

Name	Eye colour	Hair colour	Height (cm)	Wears glasses	Shoe size
Iain	blue	brown	140	✓	5
Jack	brown	ginger	142	✗	4
Kelly	green	blonde	139	✓	3
Liam	brown	black	141	✗	5
Mark	brown	brown	143	✓	5
Nicole	blue	ginger	140	✗	3

How many of the friends

(i)   have ginger hair   (1)

(ii)   wear shoes smaller than size 5   (1)

(iii)   have brown eyes and do not wear glasses   (1)

(iv)   are taller than Liam?   (1)

What fraction of the friends

(v)   wear glasses   (1)

(vi)   have black hair and brown eyes?   (1)

Challenge 6A

You might like to make a similar table to the one above for recording data about your classmates, friends or family. Any number of people would be fine but between 6 and 12 is probably best.

Make up a few questions similar to those in question 6.01

6.02 Study the information in the table in question 6.01.

(i) In the Carroll diagram below, Mark (M) and Nicole (N) have been represented by their initial letters. Complete a copy of the diagram to include all the friends in the table. (2)

	brown hair	not brown hair
brown eyes	M	
not brown eyes		N

(ii) If the friends were arranged in a line, in order of increasing height, which two would be at the ends of the line? (1)

(iii) What is the range of heights? (1)

(iv) The friends are playing a game.

Mark is blindfolded and has to guess the identity of one of his friends by asking three questions, to which the answer is 'yes' or 'no'. The questions he asks, and the answers given, are:

● Do you wear glasses?   Yes

● Are you taller than Liam?   No

● Are your eyes blue?   No

Who is the mystery friend? (2)

6.03 The tally chart below shows the numbers of cars of four colours which passed the school gate during one hour.

Car colour	Tally
black	卌 卌 卌 卌 卌 //
red	卌 卌 卌 ///
silver	卌 卌 卌 卌 卌 卌 卌 卌 卌 /
blue	卌 卌 卌 卌 ////

(i) How many cars were black? (1)

(ii) How many cars were silver? (1)

(iii) How many cars were there in total? (2)

Write down the ratio, in its simplest form, of

(iv) number of red cars : number of black cars (1)

(v) number of red cars : number of blue cars. (1)

6.04 Bertie has a collection of eight beetles, as shown in the diagram below.

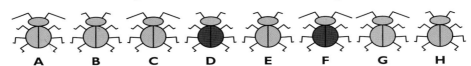

A   B   C   D   E   F   G   H

(i)   What fraction of Bertie's beetles have long antennae?   (1)

(ii)   How many of the beetles have short antennae and orange bodies?   (1)

Bertie has made a key to help him to identify his beetles.

1.	Does it have an orange body?	5.	Does it have a black body?
	Yes: go to 2		Yes: go to 6
	No: go to 5		No: go to 7
2.	Does it have long antennae?	6.	Does it have long antennae?
	Yes: go to 3		Yes: the beetle is **type T**
	No: go to 4		No: the beetle is **type U**
3.	Does it have a grey head?	7.	Does it have long antennae?
	Yes: the beetle is **type P**		Yes: the beetle is **type V**
	No: the beetle is **type Q**		No: the beetle is **type W**
4.	Does it have a grey head?		
	Yes: the beetle is **type R**		
	No: the beetle is **type S**		

Use the key to identify the **type** of

(iii)   beetle A   (1)

(iv)   beetle B   (1)

(v)   beetle C   (1)

(vi)   beetle D.   (1)

Challenge 6B

You might like to make an identification key, similar to the one above, which could be used to identify all of the classmates, friends or family whose data you recorded in Challenge 6A on page 96

You could also perhaps record some of the data in a Venn diagram like the one at the top of the next page.

6.05 Bertie decides to group all the beetles in his collection (see question 6.04) in a Venn diagram.

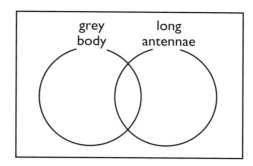

(i)   On a copy of the Venn diagram, write the letters of all of the beetles in the correct regions.   (4)

(ii)   How many of the beetles have long antennae but not grey bodies?   (1)

(iii) How many beetles have either a grey body or long antennae, but not both?   (1)

6.06 The flow chart below can be used to sort quadrilaterals into groups.

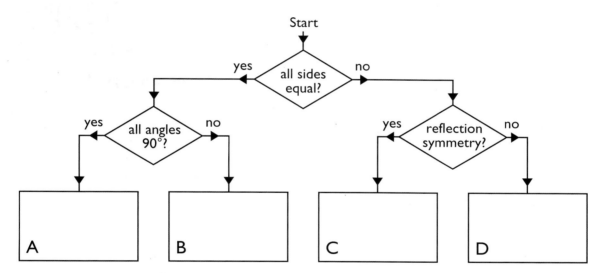

Write the letter of the rectangular box into which each of the following quadrilaterals would go.

(i)   rhombus   (1)

(ii)   rectangle   (1)

(iii) kite   (1)

(iv)   parallelogram   (1)

(v)   isosceles trapezium   (1)

(vi)   square   (1)

6.07 Ismael has started to draw the Venn diagram on the right to show the results of a school survey into pets.

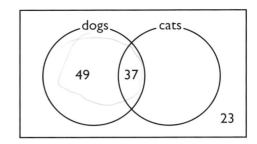

(i)   How many students keep both dogs and cats? (1)

(ii)   How many students keep dogs? (1)

The total number of students who do not keep dogs is 75

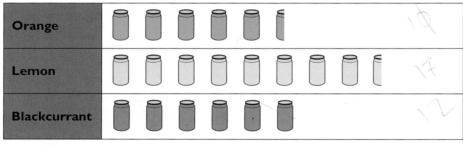

(iii)   Complete a copy of Ismael's diagram by writing the number in the remaining region. (1)

(iv)   How many students took part in the survey? (1)

(v)   How many students keep cats? (1)

(vi)   How many students keep just one type of pet? (1)

6.08 James drew the pictogram below to show the numbers of fruit drinks sold on Saturday.

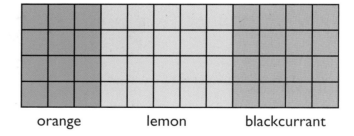

Key: ▯ represents 2 drinks.

On Saturday

(i)   how many orange drinks were sold (1)

(ii)   what was the total number of drinks sold? (1)

On Sunday, James drew the fraction diagram on the right to show the types of the 48 drinks sold.

orange   lemon   blackcurrant

On Sunday

(iii)   how many lemon drinks did he sell (1)

(iv)   what fraction, in its simplest form, of the drinks sold were blackcurrant? (1)

(v)   On which day, Saturday or Sunday, was the higher proportion of orange drinks sold? (1)

(vi)   Explain your answer to part (iii) (a). (1)

6.09 Aileen kept a tally of the number of birds that landed on her bird feeder during her 10 minute coffee break each day. She drew the bar chart below to illustrate this.

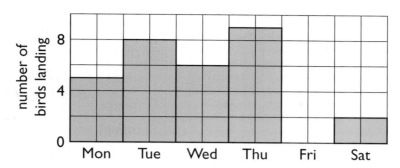

How many birds landed on the feeder on

(i)   Wednesday   (1)

(ii)   Friday?   (1)

Considering the numbers of birds landing on the six days, Monday to Saturday, what was the

(iii)   total   (1)

(iv)   range   (1)

(v)   median   (1)

(vi)   mean?   (1)

6.10 The block graph below shows the number of each type of coin in Corrie's purse.

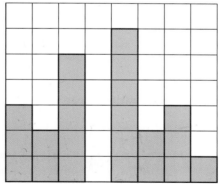

Key: One block represents 1 coin.

(i)   How many 5p coins are there?   (1)

(ii)   What is the total value of the 20p coins?   (1)

(iii)   What is the total value of all the coins?   (2)

(iv)   Using the smallest number of coins, which extra coins does Corrie need to make the total value up to £10.00?   (2)

6.11 The pie chart below shows the proportions of chocolates, mints, fudges and toffees in a box of 24 sweets.

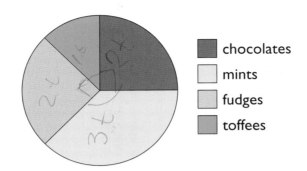

There are three times as many mints as there are toffees.

How many of the sweets are

(i)   chocolates   (1)

(ii) toffees   (1)

(iii) mints?   (1)

(iv) What percentage of the sweets are chocolates?   (1)

(v)   What fraction of the sweets are mints?   (1)

(vi) What is the ratio of the number of chocolates to the number of mints, in its simplest form?   (1)

6.12 Niamh has a square spinner with the sections numbered as shown.

She has spun the spinner 40 times and made a note of the scores on a piece of paper.

3 1 4 2 4 3 2 1 4 2 1 3 2 4 2 1 1 3 4 2
2 2 3 1 2 1 4 4 3 1 2 1 4 1 3 1 2 4 1 3
✓ ✓ ✓ ✓

Niamh has started to make a tally chart by recording the first four columns.

Score	Tally of individual scores	Frequency
1	//	
2	///	
3	//	
4	/	

(i)   Copy and complete the tally chart above.   (2)

(ii) What is the modal score?   (1)

(iii) What is the median score?   (1)

(iv) What is the mean score?   (2)

Challenge 6C

You might like to make your own square spinner and carry out a practical investigation.

6.13 The numbers of goals scored by St Germain's hockey team in the matches of the first half of term are:

2   4   1   5   3   4   0   3   4   6

    (i)   How many matches were played?   (1)

    (ii)   In how many matches did the team score more than three goals?   (1)

    (iii)   What was the median score?   (1)

    (iv)   What was the modal score?   (1)

    (v)   How many goals did the team score in total?   (1)

    (vi)   What was the mean number of goals they scored in a match?   (1)

6.14 The diagram below shows the marks achieved by a group of candidates on two papers in a maths exam.

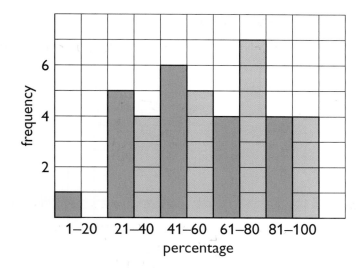

The Paper 1 results are shaded grey and the Paper 2 results are shaded orange.

How many candidates

    (i)   scored 61 or more on Paper 1   (1)

    (ii)   took the exams?   (1)

What was the modal class for

    (iii)   Paper 1   (1)

    (iv)   Paper 2?   (1)

    (v)   Suggest an explanation for the differences between the marks on the two papers.   (1)

    (vi)   For Paper 1, in which class will the median individual score lie?   (1)

6.15 The spelling test scores of ten pupils were   8   5   6   7   8   4   9   8   4   5

For this set of marks, write down the

(i)   range   (1)

(ii)   mode   (1)

(iii)   median   (2)

(iv)   mean.   (2)

6.16 The table below gives information about five friends.

Name	Age (years:months)	Height (metres)	Mass (kilograms)
Ulrika	11:8	1.36	40.2
Wilhelm	11:5	1.41	38.8
Victoria	11:4	1.44	44.5
Yale	11:1	1.39	51.5
Zac	11:7	1.40	39.0

For this group of friends, what is

(i)   the mean mass   (2)

(ii)   the mean height   (2)

(iii)   the mean age?   (2)

Can you think of an easy way to answer this last question which doesn't involve adding all the years and months?

6.17 This line graph shows Adam's journey from home to visit Eve at her house, and his journey home.

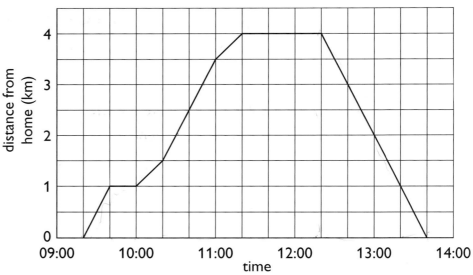

At what time did Adam

(i)   start his journey towards Eve's house   (1)

(ii)   reach home at the end of his visit?   (1)

How long was Adam

(iii)   at Eve's house   (1)

(iv)   away from home?   (1)

(v)   How far from Eve's house did Adam stop for a rest?   (1)

(vi)   On his journey home, how far did Adam walk in the hour between 12:20 and 13:20?   (1)

6.18 The line graph below shows the depth of water in a rainwater butt one afternoon.

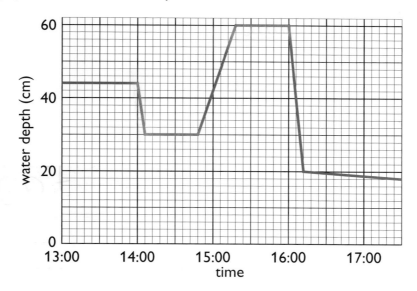

(i) What was the depth of water in the butt at 13:00? (1)

Starting at 14:00, Fred took water from the butt to water his plants.

(ii) By how many centimetres did the water level fall? (1)

(iii) For how many minutes did Fred take water? (1)

It started to rain 42 minutes after Fred stopped taking water from the butt.

(iv) At what time did it stop raining? (1)

(v) For how many minutes did the rain fall? (1)

Fred decided to top up his fishpond, starting at 16:00 and finishing at 16:12

(vi) Suggest what might explain the line showing the water level in the butt from 16:12 onwards. (1)

6.19 In Wannabeland, the unit of currency is the klop. At the start of Mia's holiday, the exchange rate was 2 Wannabeland klops (**K**) to the UK pound (£).

(i) How many klops did Mia receive for £200? (1)

Mia bought a chocolate bar for **K**1.1, a hair clip for **K**0.2 and a pair of sunglasses for **K**12.7

For these three items, what was

(ii) the total cost in klops (1)

(iii) the equivalent cost in pounds? (1)

Just before Mia left Britain, the same chocolate bar was priced at 65 pence.

(iv) In which country was it better value, and by how much in each currency unit? (1)

By the time Mia was ready to come home, the exchange rate had changed to **K**2.5 to £1 and Mia had **K**55 left to change back into pounds.

(v) How much did Mia receive when she changed the money back into pounds? (2)

6.20 The conversion graph below converts masses in kilograms (kg) to masses in pounds (lb).

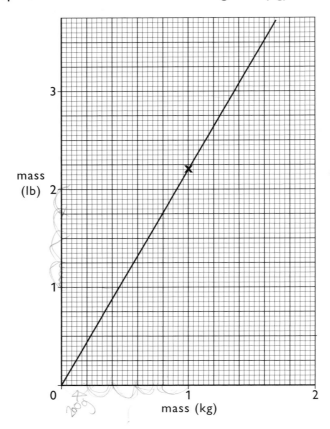

Use the graph to find the equivalent mass in pounds, to the nearest 0.1 lb, of

(i)   800 g   (1)

(ii)   1.1 kg.   (1)

Find the equivalent mass in kilograms, to the nearest 0.1 kg, of

(iii)   3 lb   (1)

(iv)   1.2 lb.   (1)

(v)   Rosie's recipe book tells her to weigh out 1 lb 8 oz of flour but Rosie's scales are
        only marked in kilograms and grams. What mass should Rosie weigh out?   (2)

Challenge 6D

W 19   You might like to find out a current exchange rate, such as from British pounds (£) to
        USA dollars ($), and draw your own conversion graph.

Although calculators can now make life easier, conversion graphs can still be very useful.

You might like to draw a graph which would help you to convert marks out of 15 to
percentages.

6.2 PROBABILITY

Questions including

● **likelihood**
● **the probability scale**
● **outcomes of events, including outcomes of two events happening at the same time**

6.21 Write down the likelihood of each of the events below happening, choosing your answers from:

impossible   very unlikely   unlikely   even chance

likely   very likely   certain

During the next week, you will

(i)   eat a bag of crisps   (1)

(ii)   see an elephant   (1)

(iii)   become 5 cm taller   (1)

(iv)   grow older.   (1)

If you roll an ordinary die, you will get

(v)   an even number   (1)

(vi)   a 6   (1)

6.22 Sukrit has the fair ordinary die and fair pentagonal spinner shown below.

Sukrit rolls the die.

[W 20] On a copy of the probability scale below, mark with the letter indicated the probability that Sukrit will score

(i)   3 (A)   (1)

(ii)   a number less than 5 (B)   (1)

(iii)   a square number (C).   (1)

```
0                               1
|___|___|___|___|___|___|___|
```

Sukrit spins the spinner.

On a copy of the probability scale below, mark with the letter indicated the probability that Sukrit will score

(iv)   1 (D)   (1)

(v)   2 (E)   (1)

(vi)   4 (F).   (1)

```
0                       1
|___|___|___|___|___|
```

6.23 (a) Niall has a square spinner and a 50p coin.

He spins the spinner and tosses the coin at the same time.

Make an organised list of the different possible outcomes.   (3)

(b) Barbara has written the letters of her name on cards.

Barbara shuffles the cards and takes one without looking.

(i) Which letter is she most likely to take?   (1)

The card she took was a letter A. She replaces the A and takes another card.

(ii) Which letter is she most likely to take this time?   (1)

The second card she took was a letter A. This time she does *not* replace the A.
She takes another card.

(iii) Is the likelihood of taking a letter A this time more likely, less likely or the
same as last time?   (1)

6.24 Diana has a pair of fair ordinary dice.

She rolls the dice at the same time and adds the scores. Write **true** or **false** for each of
these statements.

(i) The lowest possible total is 2   (1)

There is the same likelihood of getting

(ii) two 3s as there is of getting two 6s   (1)

(iii) a total of 2 as there is of getting a total of 12   (1)

(iv) a total of 2 as there is of getting a total of 5   (1)

There is an even chance of getting

(v) two even numbers   (1)

(vi) one even number and one odd number.   (1)

6.25 Katerina has made the two triangular spinners shown below.

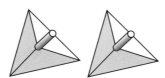

(i)   Copy and complete the table below showing all the possible outcomes of spinning both spinners at the same time. (2)

	Orange	White	Grey
Orange	OO	OW	
White	WO		
Grey	GO		

On a copy of the probability scale below, mark with the letter indicated the probabilities of the following outcomes.

0   1

(ii)   one orange, one white (A)   (1)

(iii) two orange (B)   (1)

(iv) two of the same colour (C)   (1)

(v)   neither spinner lands on orange (D)   (1)

6.26 Sam has four identical $1 coins.

Sam tosses one coin.

(i)   On a copy of the probability scale below, mark with a letter A the probability that the coin will show heads.   (1)

0   1

Sam now tosses two coins at the same time.

(ii)   How many possible outcomes are there?   (1)

(iii) On your copy, mark with a letter B the probability that both coins will show heads.   (1)

Sam now tosses three coins at the same time.

(iv) How many possible outcomes are there?   (1)

(v)   On your copy, mark with a letter C the probability that all three coins will show heads.   (1)

(vi) Which of the following do you think might be the *approximate* likelihood of getting 20 heads if 20 coins are tossed at the same time? (1)

- 1 in 20 chance
- 1 in 40 chance
- 1 in 100 chance
- 1 in 1000 chance
- 1 in a million chance

Challenge 6E

You might like to investigate probabilities!

Challenge 6F

A final challenge!

You may find that a computer will be useful here, but a hand-written version will be fine.

Choose one question from each of the 20 numbered sections 1.1 to 6.2 (see the Contents page) of this book.

You can number your questions 1.1, 1.2, 1.3, … up to …, 5.3, 6.1, 6.2 to match the numbered sections of the book.

For each of the 20 questions, using the printed question as a guide, make up your own, very similar question, using copies of the worksheets where appropriate. You can achieve this by changing names, numbers and so on. Make sure that the questions 'work' and, of course, that you know the answers!

When you have finished, you will have a test of 20 questions on a selection of the ideas throughout the book.

This is a helpful way of reminding yourself of the various topics covered in this book.

It would be a good idea to have your test checked by a teacher or parent before trying it out on your friends!